R(to)OAD
Nitmiluk

MARTIN KARI

ISBN: 978-1-63950-356-8 (sc)
ISBN: 978-1-63950-357-5 (hc)
ISBN: 978-1-63950-358-2 (e)

Writers Apex

Gateway Towards Success

8063 MADISON AVE #1252
Indianapolis, IN 46227
+13176596889
www.writersapex.com

CONTENTS

Reviews vii
Dedication ix
Preface xi

Beginning the Journey 1
South East Queensland 1
Toowoomba 4

Going Out West 6
Chinchilla 6
Roma 8
Bunya Mountains 10
Carnarvon National Park 10
Charleville 11

Northward Bound 14
Birdsville 14
Tambo 15
Barcaldine 18
Longreach 21
Winton 23
Kynuna 25
Cloncurry 29
Fountain Spring 30
Mount Isa 31
Camooweal 35

Northern Territory 39
Barkly Homestead 39
The Three Ways 41
Telegraph Station 42
Tennant Creek 43
Barrow Creek 46
The Devil's Marbles 47

Alice Springs 52

The Todd River 54

Ayers Rock 56

The Mutitjulu Story 64

Kata Tjuta – The Olgas 67

Macdonnell Ranges 71

King's Canyon 71

Hermannsburg 72

Northbound to the Top End **75**

Ti Tree 78

Tennant Creek 81

Dunmarra 86

Mataranka 87

Katherine 93

Nitmiluk National Park - Katherine Gorge 96

Kimberley Region 101

Emerald Springs 105

Darwin 108

Howard Springs 114

Berry Springs 115

The Wildlife Park 117

Litchfield National Park 120

Kakadu 126

Jabiru 131

Nourlangi Rock (Burrunguy) 132

Ubirr 137

Pine Creek 142

Termite Mound Country 142

Southbound **146**

Larrimah 146

The Three Ways 149

Eastbound to Queensland **150**

Camooweal 150

Cloncurry and the Royal Flying Doctor Service 153

Richmond 155

Torrens Creek 158

North Queensland 161

Charters Towers 161

Townsville 162

Magnetic Island 166

Northbound 168

Tea Plantation Visit 170

Atherton Tablelands 172

Coffee Works Visit 176

Mango Winery Visit 178

Kuranda 181

Nature's Cathedral 186

Cairns And Surroundings 191

Black Mountain National Park 194

Southbound 199

Townsville 199

Homeward Bound 201

Sunshine Coast - Back Home 207

Epilogue 211

About the Author 213

Back Cover Blurb 215

REVIEWS

Having had the pleasure of reading Mr. Kari's other travelogues, it is clear that he is a writer with a gift of insight, vivid memory and humanity.

It's like reading postcards from a family friend-you can almost taste the food, see the clear blue skies and feel the humidity. Reading this book is the closest you can get me to sensing the Aussie Outback without physically travelling there.

Wendy O'Hanlon, Acres Australia.

DEDICATION

For Arja Kari

To my beloved wife, Arja —

Through every winding road and quiet sunset, you have been my anchor and my compass. This journey, like so many in our lives together, was shaped by your patience, your steady courage, and your unwavering love.

When the heat of the outback pressed down, your presence brought comfort. When the road stretched endlessly before us, your laughter gave it meaning. You have been more than a travelling companion — you have been my partner in every challenge, my joy in every discovery, and my reminder that home is not a place, but a heart we share.

This book is dedicated to you, whose strength, wisdom, and light have guided me not only to Nitmiluk, but through the greatest journey of all — our life together.

With all my love,

Martin

PREFACE

Road to Nitmiluk

'All roads lead to Rome' and so they do to Nitmiluk. There are many different ways to reach a destination. So how will this journey lead to Nitmiluk, a beautiful national park in the Northern Territory?

It is a journey into the outback of Australia, where, in this oldest part of our world, nature has, throughout history, left oases of surprises in the midst of seemingly dry, barren country. One of these many oases is Nitmiluk. Others are Uluru, Kata-Tjuta, and Kakadu, all in outback Australia. The journey brings us also to the Top End of the Northern Territory and tropical North Queensland.

We need to go a long way from the continent's populated southeastern corner to step into the outback and get through to the oases that the continent has preserved in unique isolation. It is always the unexpected which surprises us: land-formations, colours, special fauna and flora, dry creek-beds, hidden water reserves, incredible heat throughout summer and shivering cold on winter nights, bush fires and bright, stinging sunshine from a cloudless sky. Then, when it rains after years, water takes over, regenerating life's cycles. Most of all, the absence of a dense human population is unexpected, with only sparse communities of Australia's indigenous Aborigines.

We can still disappear in the outback. Life has always been a real challenge there. As the name 'outback' implies, it is mainly 'out' of water and 'back' from the population centres of the continent's coastline. Whoever travels into the outback will experience lean periods in its spaces. But there is also recovery, for the one who finds his way through.

Such contrasts can add to an experience. This is what makes a journey special. I have toured other parts of the world, describing them in my biography 'Journey of a Lifetime' Volumes 1 and 2. Now you, the reader, are welcome to join me and follow the 'Road to Nitmiluk', retracing this great journey.

BEGINNING THE JOURNEY

SOUTH EAST QUEENSLAND

Being experienced world travellers, and after twenty years in Australia, we (myself and my wife Arja) decided to explore the beautiful but more isolated parts of this great country. We decided to travel the road to Nitmiluk – a national park in the Northern Territory. The children had started to lead their own lives, giving us some time for learning a bit more about this unique continent of Australia, which is dominated by its outback. Fourteen thousand kilometres lay ahead of us before we would return home to Caboolture, just north of Brisbane in South East Queensland.

One of our destinations, Darwin, had its own significance for us as our youngest daughter Gucki was studying music at the Northern Territory University. We wanted to be present later on for her first concert. Another reason to celebrate was my sixtieth birthday, celebrated shortly before our starting date on the 21st July 2001. As long as we aim for something special in our lives, reasons can always be found to support it.

Success at many things we undertake in our lives depends heavily on preparation. The outback is unforgiving and doesn't allow much room for failure. A strong sense of independence coupled with a good health-status becomes the basis for early planning and preparation. The condition of the car cannot be stressed enough; it is absolutely vital. Travelling by car on your own gives such an adventure a special significance: the greater the challenge the greater the rewards.

Timing of an outback trip is also important; it is best in the beginning or end of the Australian winter (May-June / August -September), when temperatures are not too high and heavy rain is more unlikely. Having said this, in the Northern Territory alone, we experienced, in the winter month of July, a temperature difference of 41 degrees Celsius in the shade through the day and - 5 degrees Celsius at night. Car air-conditioning can help for a limited time, but not for a whole day and night!

A closed hood rack on the car top will not only carry your gear but also help to break the sun's force, which otherwise penetrates the car's interior. Water on board is as important as spare petrol for the car. A bull-bar fitted on the front of the car can protect from sudden wildlife incursions onto the road. A good variety of food properly stored away, a selection of tools including a shovel, map material, sleeping facilities (in our case a self-inflatable mattress in the back of the car), fly screens on at least two opposite windows, personal items like a diary, reading material, photo equipment, insect repellent spray and a basic medical first-aid kit should also not be forgotten. A mobile phone will have only limited use as most of the outback was out of the reception area at the time of our tour.

Having attended to all these issues, we were ready now for the big adventure. The driver is as important as the car; a better car cannot replace an unskilled driver. A four-wheel drive is not a necessity for this tour; but it can be useful to have in case it is needed.

Before leaving in early morning darkness, we pinned written instructions on the fridge door for our youngest son Micki. 'After school each day feed the cats, dogs, donkeys, parrots and don't forget yourself! Plants on the veranda need watering once a week. On Fridays see the neighbour to help you with the shopping.' Everything at home was secured as far as it could be. We crossed our fingers as our car with camper trailer behind rolled out of the property gate.

Camper trailer test at home

Car accommodation test

In the early hours of the day, the sleeping city of Brisbane was still waiting for the traffic. Going south, the mountains of the Great Dividing Range blocked the coastal area. Ancient rainforest hung on the mountain slopes. Its tall dense leaf-canopy turns the sky into darkness even during the day; lianas swing around massive tree trunks climbing higher and higher. Further up, huge granite formations take over in Girraween National Park, which we left in the south, before heading west.

TOOWOOMBA

The road climbs up to the eagle eyrie of Toowoomba, where first daylight welcomed us to a town just waking up. Crisp, cold air was still all around, but a clear sky allowed the sun to shine through as the day progressed. The city is home to the Carnival of Flowers - a spring festival in September where gardens and parks are drenched in a sea of colour as carefully cultivated plants bloom. Toowoomba's highland position makes it a magnificent place to live with a more moderate climate than directly on the coast.

Views to the coast are surrounded by rainforests on mountain-slopes. The open country to the west makes Toowoomba the border town to the endless Outback.

Road trains of the Outback stop here; their sizes don't fit city traffic any more, but in the Outback they are 'kings of the road', demanding appropriate respect from all drivers. These road trains travel long distances carrying loads of livestock, goods or crops.

Sign into the outback

GOING OUT WEST

The road to the west opened views far to the horizon; the land with the fields dropped away slightly. In between, old volcanic formations stuck out of the flat land; green eucalypt forests climbed up to the 'pancake' top, indicating a prehistoric volcanic crater. As a result of this ancient landmark, the black soil here supports one of the best agricultural areas of Australia.

CHINCHILLA

Further west, the town of Chinchilla was entirely surrounded by fields, in which the yellow and brown colours of the dry winter season became more dominant the further the road led to the horizon. Green fields appeared only where irrigation from underground water was in use. This is a fact not just here, but throughout the outback.

Exact information on long-term water usage is not yet available. Despite the size of the underground artesian basin, it is not known if this level is restored sufficiently through yearly precipitation to maintain supply. Neither is it known what our interference does to the water quality. In Western Australia, seawater entered from somewhere to make up for the lost water pumped out of the artesian basin. This contaminated the rest of the water. Australia has to manage its small water reserves in a specific water-wise way. For this mainly dry continent, the future of the country depends on it.

Chinchilla invited visitors to have a rest at the local petrol station on a fresh green lawn with a table and benches around. The entrance to a timber house was lined on both sides by the typical Queensland Bottle tree. Its tribute to the Outback was the wide bottle-shaped grey-green trunk and the dense leafy green canopy.

Chinchilla – S.W. Qld

Bottle trees call the Outback their home; they store water in their trunks for years and therefore always look green. They are also drought, flood, fire and sub-zero temperature resistant - a really tough Aussie!

Shortly after we arrived in Chinchilla, a local joined us - a tall, slim, elderly man stopped to water a perfect lawn area with a hose. This lawn was the only one that could be seen along the road in Chinchilla.

"Where are you from? You must be city-folk visiting our country. We haven't had the rain you've had on the coast. Look how dry everything is."

"But your place looks beautiful."

"The artesian water is no good for us any more and soon it will be the same for the crops in the fields. In my eighty years of life, I have never seen the place so dry. Past droughts regularly received a break with the wet summer season bringing rain. Now this doesn't seem to happen any more. If this doesn't change, there will be no future in the country any more. No wonder our younger generation moves to the city. The country has always supported the city. What will the city do without this support?"

"You still have a long way to go from what you say. In our early days we could not even dream about a tour through our Outback."

"Anyway, my flowers are begging me for water and I better not let them down. Their colours look so beautiful, don't they? Have a good trip; look after yourselves and respect our country."

ROMA

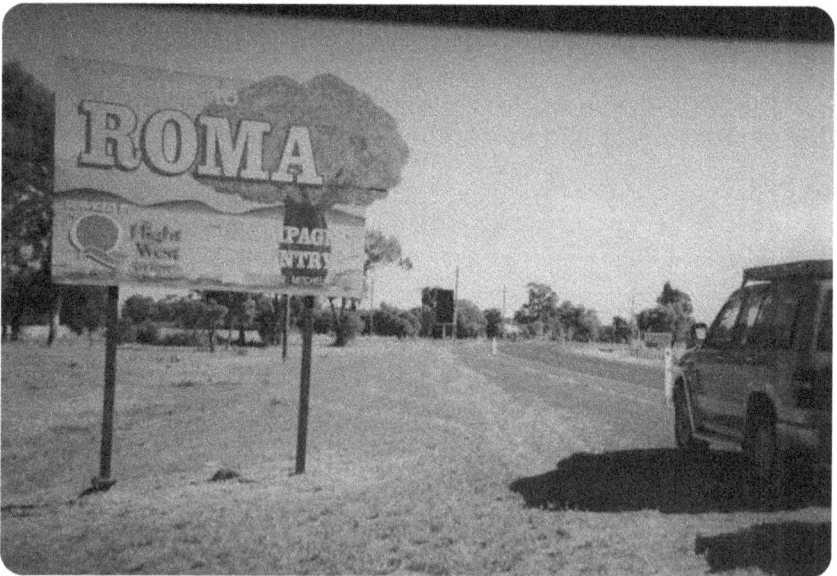

Roma – S.W. Qld

Our next destination further west was Roma. The land is flat to the horizon. A blue sky spans large, freshly fallowed fields. These fields were ready to start the winter crops. Unfortunately, the absence of cloud predicted there would be no rain, which the land needed desperately for a harvest. Agricultural machinery, new and old, sat idle around the railway station, waiting for its part of the work in the endless fields.

The number of houses told of a rather small community, dominated by a number of high rising wheat silos next to the railway line. Queensland-style houses on tall stumps were everywhere. Their unique style allowed the much-needed air circulation during the summer heat. They were less ornately built than many Queenslanders near coastal towns. The timber built houses here had fewer verandas, which was indicative of a tighter financial situation in the area.

After the prevalent cedar forests along the coast had been widely decimated in the past, new cypress plantations were started, especially around Roma. This diversified the local farming activities. Only the older houses were cedar and silky oak constructions, which are termite-proof and last a long time if properly built. Cypress was introduced to replace these sturdy timbers of the past, because it grows in the harsh dry conditions of the west.

Termites (white ants) are strong co-inhabitants in most parts of Australia. There is not much timber around any more that termites cannot decompose. Cypress is nowhere near as good as the cedar of the past. However, its cultivation brought to the outback an additional income for the farming communities. Timber farming is a step in the right direction for the protection of the natural forest growth, which is mainly only found now in the eastern coastal areas of the continent.

BUNYA MOUNTAINS

One of the oases in the outback is the area closer to the coast between Kingaroy and Dalby, the Bunya Mountains. On this tour we didn't pass through the area, but because of its unique nature, it is worth mentioning. In the middle of flat country, a densely forested mountain ridge rises.

Here the outstanding pine species, the Bunya Pine, grows majestically. Nature has supplied the Bunya Pine with an oasis, where it has survived since prehistoric times. Visiting such an area is like going back millions of years in time. In three-year-cycles, the Bunya Pines develop huge, spiky cones during December and January. When they drop, they can be very dangerous. At these times, the area is often closed to visitors. The nuts nestled in the cone are nutritious when properly prepared. During the Bunya season, the Aborigines would temporarily set aside their tribal differences and gather in the mountains for great Bunya Nut feasts.

The strong ancient growth of these trees in a forest oasis of their own gives an impression of how nature can sometimes survive in isolation. From the top of the Bunya Mountains, the vastness of the Australian continent can only be guessed at. Across the dark green treetops there lies the yellow-brown and reddish sunburnt land.

CARNARVON NATIONAL PARK

Further west of Roma, a road led to the north into one of the mountain ranges of the Great Dividing Range. This bush-forest retreat with a natural water reservoir surrounded by mighty, colourful rock walls was Carnarvon National Park.

Carnarvon National Park – S.W. Qld

The green flora was unexpected. It was another outback-oasis where precious water invites the visitor to a refreshing swim in summer, something not very common in the Australian outback. Here, the total peace is uninterrupted by predators like the crocodiles in the north of the continent. The trip from Roma took three to four hours on a dusty beaten track. During sudden storms in summer the road can become partly cut off, leaving travellers stranded. This can happen in many places in the outback, which is why travellers need enough reserves to be able to survive in reasonable comfort.

CHARLEVILLE

Before Charleville, we had taken the road to the north. Now, to continue our journey, we had to come back all the way to Roma after a lonely visit to Carnarvon National Park. Between dry grassland was the evergreen bush, holding more and more wildlife. In the distance, emus - rarely more than two together - stuck their small heads supported by long necks out of the high grass. During the day they are on the run where the road comes closer to their territory and then develop quite a speed over a distance with their heads remaining above the grass. When young, emus look beautiful in their brown-yellow stripes. However, as adults they don't reach the splendour of their larger African colleagues, the ostrich. The harsher conditions in Australia limit the emus to a smaller size and their plumage looks rather rough as befits an inhabitant of these harsh conditions.

Kangaroos moving towards the road don't watch the traffic, so it is necessary to watch for new green grass, which comes up to the side of the road. The grass is mainly kept fairly short along the sides of the road allowing new grass to shoot well. The dew that runs off the road at night assists it to grow. Early morning and evening hours is the time when kangaroos move - sometimes great distances - on the lookout for feeding grounds. They don't read traffic signs; roads encroach on their territory, so a driver has to watch resting and moving kangaroos carefully.

When they become unsettled, kangaroos can jump distances up to six metres using their strong back legs, making it dangerous for traffic on the road. They can jump out of the bush suddenly and hit the front of your car, often making it impossible to stop in time. The resulting impact can only be minimised with a mounted bull-bar on the front of the car. Caution remains the best protection, because in a few cases, when a larger Red Kangaroo is hit by a bull-bar it doesn't land on the road, but comes up through the windscreen, causing not only considerable damage, but inflicting serious injuries to car passengers when it punches around with its hoofs in its agony. Dead kangaroos on the road are a constant reminder of this peril.

Besides kangaroos, wild black boars can occasionally be seen. Early European settlers introduced them just as they did rabbits, creating unwanted problems today in the fragile Australian bush, which is not prepared for hosting scavengers. Australia has become a peaceful eco-system through its isolation, leaving its species to live together without the hunting skills required for their survival. This is one of the many facts that make Australia a special place. It is hoped that Australia's society will adapt to its nature and there can be a peaceful coexistence.

NORTHWARD BOUND

As we kept on the road to the north, the land further west, where the outback becomes even more distinct, was by-passed. Our next stop was to be Birdsville. Small places like Birdsville on the border to South Australia could be reached only by dirt road. The land is dead flat; bushes have problems hanging on in this semi-desert environment.

BIRDSVILLE

Birdsville has record summer temperatures and one event in August keeps the place with its small population alive. The Birdsville Races take place far away from coastal areas, where horse races are more common. Once a year, the 'coast' comes to this ooftenutback event. During the week's races, visitors easily outnumber the local population. Somebody who wants to experience real outback characters can find them here, in remote Birdsville.

Our route followed the Great Dividing Ranges, which keep the grasslands and the bush fairly lush in the lower area through its climatic influence. The further west, the more such influence retreats, the more it opens the door to semi-desert. Most inland parts of Australia can maintain bush vegetation with the exemption of specific desert areas such as the Simpson, Great Victoria, and Great Sandy Deserts. They are not deserts like the Libyan Desert, which is known for its endless sand dunes. Life has managed to 'hang around' in many forms in Australian desert areas. If not visible, it is often hiding underground: root-plants, snakes, lizards, bandicoots, and bilbies.

TAMBO

Our next stop was Tambo. Despite being clearly marked on the map, it was so small that only the caravan park on the side of the road flagged its existence. Places to stay overnight are well documented in most tourist guides. A caravan park usually offers both caravans and cabins for accommodation, but you can also bring your own and in most cases cooking and shower facilities are available for a reasonable price.

Just before the Tambo caravan park, a kangaroo nearly jumped into our car. Luckily, we had started to slow down earlier as darkness had moved in. The temperature changed to cold very quickly as the sun disappeared beyond the horizon. Through a wide-open gate we entered the caravan park, where, under a group of old-grown acacias, other cars and caravans had taken their positions for the night. Once inside the gate, a hut to the left indicated new arrivals had to be booked in. When we arrived, the hut was empty; a sign asked instead to book yourself in and leave your caravan fees of $8 for one night in a tin-box.

People here apparently trusted others. The owner was busy with something else; in the outback, a holiday is something unknown. It is only city folk that have the luxury to go away for a break. Here, conditions keep most people on their toes, not allowing much time for a holiday. Outside the hut was a cooking facility and a room with showers. The water came from a tank high above ground and served both the shower and toilet. These facilities cost an extra dollar. A clear message told everybody, 'Be water-wise; if we run out, we all have nothing left.'

Everybody in the park had set up camp as far away as possible from the road so they would not be disturbed by the road train traffic at night.

These long, heavy, manifold trailers thundered by from time to time. We took our position closer to the road, because we didn't want to disturb others when leaving early in the morning.

Once everything was ready for the night, we joined a group of people around a fireplace. The beer went around and everybody relaxed enough to speak out freely. What surprised me was not that most retired couples came from down south, but that so many had overseas stories to tell as well. They were talking about European countries, where everybody claimed to have been. When finding out that we originally came from overseas, some showed their disappointment at not being able to impress us with any more stories.

As we sat there, it was totally silent, with no traffic on the nearby road, something that can't be experienced in and around cities. Only the licking flames of the ground fire broke the darkness under the dense canopy of the park's acacias. By keeping quiet and looking around, you could see that kangaroos had come just to the edge of the group where shadows formed. A number of kangaroos sat right up on their strong back legs, supported by their tails on the ground in a comfortable position. They were only visible by their lighter underneath fell. Their pointed ears moved constantly keeping them on constant guard.

We noticed too that an owl snared a feast of a mouse that it intercepted in a nosedive from high in an acacia. Bats cut their passage above the trees and became visible only where the sky shone with its stars through the trees' canopy. Ants on the ground didn't miss joining in; the legendary outback flies kept away because of the cold winter night. Never before-heard strange sounds reached the attentive ear. Nobody could tell what the sounds indicated - was it anxiety, a warning or pleasure? The crickets' chirping was missing because it was winter; in summer they can disrupt a night's silence.

A scent in the air revealed the existence of flowers in the acacia trees, which could not be seen between the dark-green leaf-canopy in the darkness. Without noticing, everybody around the fireplace had stopped talking to listen to what Mother Nature had to say. Nature is still our best teacher, but we have first to learn to listen to it and obey it. Even after we moved back to our car for a night's sleep, people around the smouldering, glowing fire continued on well into the morning hours. Only our continued quiet presence in our car made a bandicoot or a bilby curious enough to come and have a look at us. Nature here is so cautious; its fauna comes out of hiding only if the conditions are right. They have learnt to assess for themselves what is necessary for their survival.

The occasional bypassing thunder of a road train didn't disturb the wildlife visitors but disrupted our sleep. In the outback, it is strongly recommended that you do not drive at night. Most of the wildlife moves to feed under the protection of the cooler night. Cattle can also become a danger in the dark if not noticed in time. Road trains have huge mounted bull-bars on the front, which they can use to forcibly remove everything in their way, while maintaining full speed. A road train cannot stop as easily as a car. Sometimes the swinging trailers behind hit an oncoming vehicle and the driver of the road train isn't always aware of it. In the outback, it is best if the road trains are respected by moving to the side or even stopping completely to let them pass.

Our next day started early after not much sleep at all. On the side of the road, kangaroos immediately showed up at daybreak. Until the brilliant, clear morning sun gradually drove out the darkness, we moved slowly, keeping a close eye on the 'roos'. A road train coming from behind made us instantly move to the side of the road and let it pass. With daylight gaining the upper hand, the 'roos' disappeared almost entirely. Were they watching the colourful spectacle of an outback sunrise like we were?

Far on the eastern horizon, where the earth bends, the darkness rose first with a band of dark-blue daylight changing from dark red to lighter colours, the higher the sun rose, then changing to yellow from dark to light until the fireball of the sun was completely over the horizon. Shadows of bush, rock, and tree followed the daylight from initially vague shapes on the ground, becoming more distinct and longer, until the sun appeared completely. With the rise of the sun, the temperature increased quickly during the morning.

BARCALDINE

Passing Blackall to Barcaldine, vast grasslands and wheat fields lined the road. Sometimes it was difficult to distinguish one from the other, as winter had dipped everything in yellow-brown colours. Barcaldine is a small outback town bearing an importance in Australian history. It was here in 1891 that the Labor Party was founded, not in a major city, but here in the outback. In commemoration of this event, a ghost-gum tree was planted almost one hundred years earlier in a special part of the town. It became the symbol of the Labor movement. The tree survived all the ups and downs of history until only recently, when the 'tree of knowledge' was poisoned. The tree is now gone, but the idea behind it still lives on.

In Barcaldine, the railway joined the road to Longreach after coming from Rockhampton on the east coast. This railway line was a vital lifeline for the Queensland outback ending in Longreach, a major town in a vast region. People used this link to the coast to stay in contact with the outer world.

When the train arrives in our hometown Caboolture from Longreach, many of the outback folk carry big luggage-bags, indicating that they have prepared themselves for this long journey to the coast. The way of thinking here is to bring on to the train everything that can be carried, because nobody can tell whether something in the luggage might be needed.

Closer to Longreach, scattered eucalypt forests and bush had been visibly destroyed. This was due to archaic legislation, which gave farmers of the area tax incentives to clear bushland every year. This must have been a way to 'buy off' farmers many years ago by encouraging them to clear land for cultivation. Today, this does not happen any more; environmental considerations have gained priority to purposeless land clearing.

Farming in the outback has always been associated with risks related to the unpredictable rainfall. Environmental changes are here to stay. We haven't managed to reverse nature's cycles, only to offset them partially. Especially in the outback, we have lessons to learn for the future.

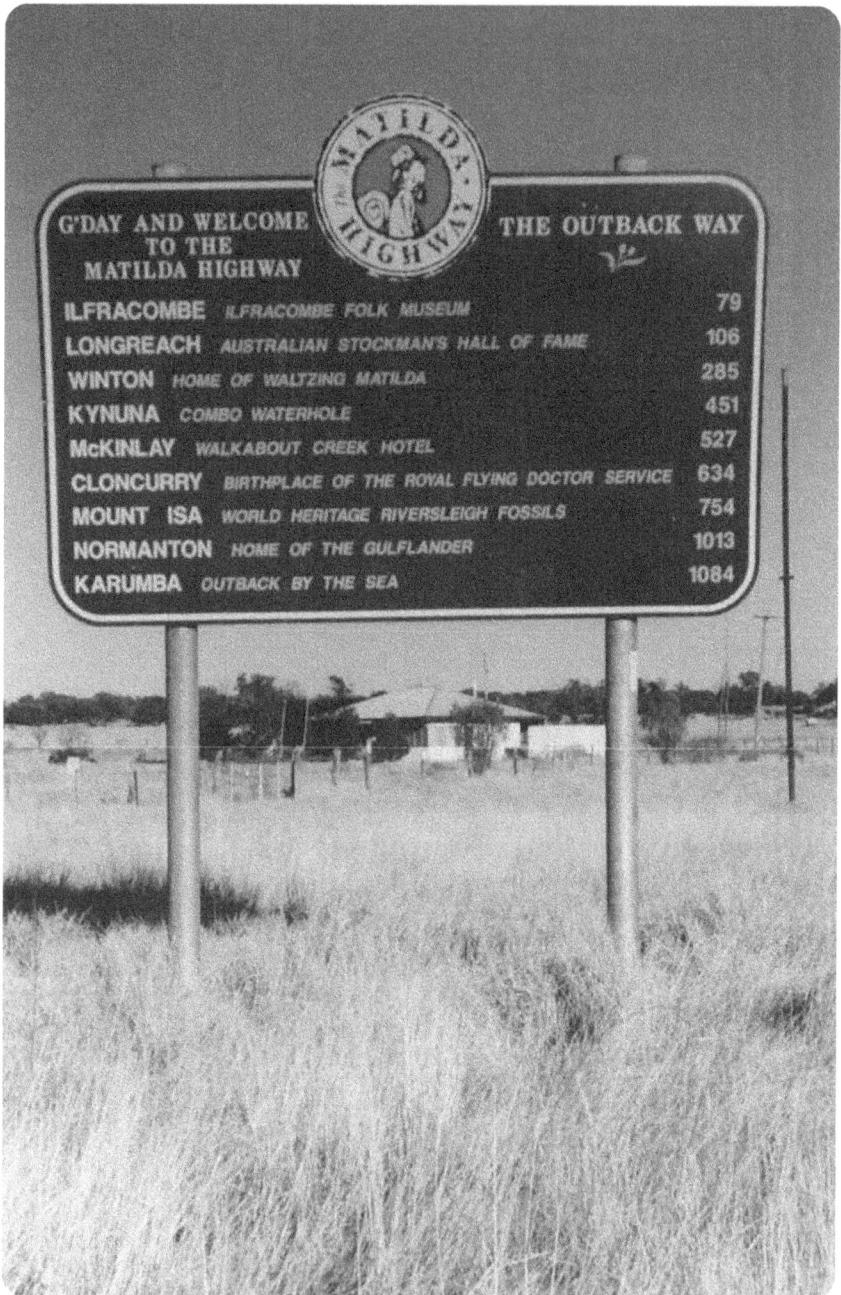

Matilda Highway road sign - outback Qld

LONGREACH

Longreach - outback Qld

Longreach has a long-standing pioneering history in Australian aviation. It was from here that QANTAS started nearly eighty years ago, one of the most successful enterprises in the country, connecting Queensland and the Northern Territory with its air services. In those early days, these flights were pioneering adventures in a vast empty continent with its extreme conditions. Today, a Hall of Fame reminds visitors of these early pioneering days.

The town temporarily diminishes the feel of the outback. Here, tree-lined avenues and frequent green lawns make you forget the harsh conditions for a while. A small park invited us to take a good rest. Anybody visiting the outback should always remember that no matter how small an achievement might seem, here it is a vital building block in a culture still in the making. There are no symbols like high-rise buildings, highways, modern housing estates, leisure and cultural institutions like we conveniently have in cities.

Living in the outback is a credit to every individual who makes it. There is space here in abundance; the rest has to be worked out individually. Time can assist in this process; there has never been anything wasted here. This didn't escape our attention at a petrol station, when a young boy asked where we came from and where we were heading. His face became melancholic when we responded, probably because he was not sure whether he would be able to make a journey like ours one day. He stood looking longingly after us as we disappeared. I could only assure him, "If you try hard enough, your dreams may one day come true."

At our resting-place opposite the Hall of Fame, a gentleman joined us with his teenaged son. As it turned out, they also came from Brisbane. The big difference was that their car had gone on strike and needed a few days work to get them back on the road. Despite the fact that we didn't need any mechanical service, we decided we would give the two blokes a lift into town to the workshop.

The job wasn't finished, but was well on the way. A timber shed was all there was to indicate the mechanical workshop. Here, anything was possible. Spare parts never caused a problem: a blacksmith's stove, welding equipment, small machining facilities plus the skill of the local mechanic created a solution for every problem. Nobody left that workshop disappointed. They got everybody going again.

"Help is vital here in the outback. We never say we cannot help."

Listening to the mechanic's words, we knew our two blokes were in good hands. People you meet in the outback are generally trustworthy. We shared our provisions with the two stranded fellows and when leaving, agreed to meet again in Alice Springs. Surprisingly, though taking different routes, this did eventuate.

WINTON

Winton, another small, typically outback town, lay ahead of us. As we drove in, we could see that there was a line of houses on each side, leaving the central area under a row of trees to provide ample parking space for horses, cars, motorbikes and everybody else who came along to have a yarn at the all important local pub. The worst possible scenario in the outback would be 'a pub with no beer.'

Winton - outback Qld

It is the pub where people meet most of the time and where news is exchanged. Through the day at the pub, we didn't meet the locals; but there were plenty of tourists experiencing that bit of outback pub atmosphere. A number of four-wheel drives were also parked in front of the pub, indicating in many cases traveller-status.

When their car was covered with mud, people were more likely to be talking about experiences on tracks going west through Boulia to Alice Springs, highly recommending the use of a four-wheel drive. A vehicle is however, not always the answer to dusty stony tracks; the driver is as important. An inexperienced driver can wreck any car; the emphasis should be on caution and knowing what not to do: for instance, speeding in unknown territory.

What can a visitor to a pub in Winton expect? When setting foot through the door, dim daylight fills the area along the bar, where light sources come from the ceiling directed towards the walls. The wall behind the bar shows a selection of bottles in glass cupboards, everything neatly exhibited. Other walls show photos of historic houses, the pub many years back, the local footy team and references to the unofficial Australian national anthem 'Waltzing Matilda'. The origin of this well known song is in Winton. No wonder that, after a couple of beers, Waltzing Matilda starts to make the rounds.

In an Australian pub everybody is considered equal; you never really know with whom you have a beer; and this is good, because it does keep the door open to any conversation. Anybody can walk in and join in a yarn or bring up his own story as long as there is respect shown to others. Towards the end of the day it is more likely that the locals turn up in the pub. The round tables with their chairs invite everyone to a typical outback dinner, which would mainly consist of a 'solid' steak from the outback cattle. A pool table next to the window closest to the roadside invites a game together with a dartboard on another wall. The TV in the top corner can be watched from anywhere in the pub, supplying the extra entertainment and noise, which fills the pub.

All this will be left behind as the outback again takes over. The contrast of total silence in the vast open spaces of the outback and the atmosphere in the pub is a worthwhile experience. Coming out of the isolation into a pub unlocks in everybody a desire to communicate and have a good time with others. It is here that the real Aussies can be met, equal 'blokes', open and helpful when needed. Then, you are ready to return to the stillness and quiet.

Typical Outback resting place

KYNUNA

The pub experience behind us, we moved on to Kynuna for the day. The whole place was made up of the petrol station and a pub with a caravan park behind it. After filling the tank of our car, I had to walk around the whole place to find the boss, a lady who took the money.

"How much petrol did you get?" she asked. I had to go back and have a look for myself to know the answer. The caravan fees were added to the cost of the fuel, allowing us to stay overnight with a few other guests under a wide acacia tree in the fenced-off area behind the pub building. The canopy of the acacia was the only green in the area. With its yellow-brown colour, the high standing grass in this flat country reflected the dry winter season. Not even the red colour of the soil showed through because everything was covered with brown-grey dust.

When we took our position in the park, the day hadn't progressed far enough for the sun to disappear behind the horizon. A sound of pounding hoofs indicated a cattle herd rushing near the fence through the grassland. One bull must have been the leader, because all the others followed his direction. This happened at the same time each day. It must have been the feed and the water waiting for them at the farm.

As the sun closed in over the horizon, it produced its daily spectacle of colours, going from light to dark red and then blue, changing to black as night closed in, allowing the stars to break through with their shine. At twilight, four large, grey birds landed on their long legs in the middle of the park. They seemed to come out of the air from nowhere, walking naturally around between the caravans and collecting food that people wrongly decided to give them. Only after the feeding frenzy had stopped, the incoming night reminded the proud strutting birds to head to their territory for the night. It was a unique experience, watching them running a distance on the ground, then lifting up with their large wings, rolling first sidewise in the air. Then, a faster stroke of their wings directed them higher and faster towards the horizon, which just showed the last glimmer of the sun along the bend of the earth.

When ready for our dinner, a magpie joined us, claiming a place on our table and regarding it as a certainty that we would feed it. Nature seemed to connect with us here. In the complete darkness of the night, a kangaroo also made itself known, the knock on the ground from its feet rushed within reach of us through the park. We must have been on its usual passage. The thunder-like sound next to us in the silent darkness gave us a bit of a fright.

After spending a cold winter night, we could not wait much longer for sunrise. With the first sign of daybreak on the horizon, we were ready to continue our outback journey. Only when leaving, we realised that we had a neighbour living in a small tent next to the fence. Its occupant was an Aborigine dressed in old suit-parts, originating from more than one suit. He seemed to be content with his outfit that showed his move more towards our societal norms. His insecurity however, left him hiding in his tent for most of the time.

7 We couldn't be sure whether he heard or understood our greeting, as he didn't respond. It was also difficult to establish his age from his appearance. His face and grey hair indicated rather an advanced age. However, their way of life in a harsh Australian environment usually ages the aborigines earlier than their white Australian counterparts. The Aborigines are losing contact with their traditional world and have problems integrating into a world of our understanding.

This Aborigine spoke only a few words to us, which we could not understand because he used his own language. Pieces of string represented some value for him. He showed me what he made out of them, while he remained in the low tent. Who should feel sorry, we for him or he for us? As long as he didn't understand our way of life, he was probably feeling sorry for us.

An immense complex issue has emerged in Australia. When dealing with indigenous people, no money can deliver the answers, rather a totally open understanding for each other's position, supported by patience. Empathy for the other culture is a priority in any attempt to get closer to each other. Our way of thinking doesn't necessarily match the indigenous way of thinking. We had other meetings with Aborigines during our tour and experience and knowledge was always gained from them.

As our 'poor looking' Aborigine from Kynuna showed me his string-work, I returned his respect with something he could easily relate to: biscuits and a tin of peaches from our stock. Firstly, he retreated, not being sure about it, but when the items were left in front of his tent and we had moved out of his way, he hastily collected it. The moment we left, he came out of the tent to our car, again saying something I unfortunately could not understand. However, his face told us he was happy about what we gave him. When I asked him via my hand movements, whether he could open the tin, he went back to the tent showing me with his knife how he would open the tin. Why was he living on his own here? Nobody could tell me. The caravan owner allowed him to stay on the land for free. At least someone had the heart to grant him a place to stay, which in his understanding was already something of an achievement. No efforts should be spared, if we want to reach others like our Kynuna aboriginal acquaintance.

Road Train - king of the outback road

Wheat Country – Outback Qld

Back on the road, where harvesting burn-off as part of widespread farming had turned the land into ashes, some of the monotonous landscape was left behind. In lower areas of hillsides, green bush returned to the scene and in the distance table-like mountains announced the highlands around Mount Isa.

CLONCURRY

Cloncurry was next on the main road, a long way from Longreach. Despite having a bitumen surface, roadsides had to be watched for sapphires that could imbed into tyres and cut their way through. We had arrived in a mineral stronghold, where a sharp eye could find valuable minerals exposed over time. On this tour, our mineral search was limited to an inspection of the tyres from time to time for imbedded sapphires, accidentally picked up on the side of the road. A small screwdriver helped to prise them out, before they could cut deeper.

The rural town of Cloncurry is a rich area of minerals. On its outskirts next to a small park there was a mineral museum exhibiting the wealth of the area. This is an 'El Dorado' for a mineral-hobbyist and it is undoubtedly one of the richest areas in the world. Just outside the museum in the open was a collection of old equipment, which was used for farming, building roads and mining. Everywhere else in the world they would have ended up in a scrap yard for recycling. Not so here in the outback, where everything has a special importance. Nothing could be easily replaced in the past; everything received a much more extended life which was demonstrated by this collection of old equipment.

Houses along the main road through Cloncurry were evidence of the Queensland housing style with houses raised on stumps, verandas and flowering gardens around the perimeters. Here, on a main arterial to the coast, materials were more readily available than further south, from where we had come.

Towards Mount Isa – N.W. Qld

The road to Mount Isa climbed constantly. Colourful rocky slopes stood out against the green bush and the yellow flowers of wattles in the midst of the severe dry season. Life always wins the battle in nature's regeneration here. Eucalypt trees also try to hang on in the rock fields, returning life to the outback. Nature displays an unexpected beauty in its struggle for survival; what is hard and takes long to build, forms character through its beauty.

FOUNTAIN SPRING

The Flinders Highway leading from Townsville on the coast to Mount Isa brought the traffic, which we hadn't seen for a while, back into the outback. Before Mount Isa though, a place called Fountain Spring turned up next to the road. Many tourists had set up camp, hardly leaving any space for a new arrival. It was amazing, how in limited places all over the country people gathered and tried to catch a little bit of their own adventure; but it is also good that everybody is to a degree different so that not all are in one and the same place at the same time. With experience, the location of a concentration of tourists could almost be predicted.

Every tourist in Fountain Spring must have looked for a fountain, which during winter was most certainly non-existent. The rugged, colourful rocky slopes with scattered vivid bush-green inspired the ones, who had their eyes open; how many times people look at something and still see nothing. German talking could be heard from within the visitors groups and came as no surprise. Germans can be found almost everywhere around the globe. Do they like to get away from their own country so much?

MOUNT ISA

After a short stop, we continued on the road to Mount Isa, leaving almost all the tourists behind in one place. Where the mountain ridge crossed the horizon, the top of a 'chimney' stuck out above it, announcing the rich mining town of Mount Isa.

Mount Isa

As soon as the road had reached this mountain ridge, the mining town lay further on in a dip. Skyrocketing 'chimneys' towered in the midst of black slagheaps, everything higher up than the housing estates, effectively blocking the expansion of the town. The mining operations are underground here: copper, lead, zinc, silver, and tungsten. Everything that is highly valuable can be found here, making Mount Isa one of the richest mining towns in the world.

The individual houses also reflect this wealth; they are all neat and tidy with flourishing gardens and air conditioning boxes to beat the enormous heat during the summer. It was hard to believe that a large number of Finnish migrants, who earned exceptionally good money, had successfully settled here from their cold native country. They even had their own Finnish clubhouse in town. Many Finns didn't need to learn much of the English language, because they were a strong community held in high esteem for their hard and reliable work. Mostly, they later retired to the Queensland coast.

Several years later as I am writing this, a note in the Finnish paper mentions that the Finnish club in Mount Isa might be shut down, because the generation of Finns from earlier days have left the work force and no more Finns have arrived to replace them. This is how the 'roulette of fortunes' turns in the world, never staying in one and the same place.

A German club indicated another strong presence at the time. It was easy to see that Mount Isa was a work place, because hardly anybody could be seen in the streets during the day or in the so important local pub. What were missing here in winter were the extreme heat and the outback flies. Eighteen years earlier as we passed through Mount Isa the first time, 45 degrees Celsius in the shade, high humidity and billions of flies made a stay in the area quite a challenge; all this plus the risks caused through floods is reason enough to refrain from travelling in the north of Australia during summer.

Aussies have developed their own ingenuity. For instance, how to tackle the problem of flies; a cowboy hat with corks on strings around the brim keeps flies out of the face when moving, depending how many flies there are. The typical Aussie hand-movement in front of the face - known as the great Australian wave - has only limited effect.

A sign in some places indicates how serious Australian outback conditions can be; 'Motorists are advised not to travel these areas during the months December-March because of extreme temperatures and hazardous driving conditions.' It is not advisable to ignore such signs. Outside of Mount Isa, large water storage was created along the Templeton River. Lake Moondarra served the area with its own facility for recreational purposes (boating, fishing, swimming) as well as the water supply.

West of Mount Isa

Past Mount Isa, the rocky, rugged mountains gradually gave way to grass and bushland. At times, the road had only little asphalt or none, exposing stones along with the dust. Driving fast here is just plain reckless, because an oncoming vehicle will inevitably have reduced vision because of a dust-cloud, suddenly throwing stones into the air. Some drivers do the right thing; they slow down, move to the side to avoid stones. Others don't and they can cause a number of problems like the very common windscreen damage. There is unfortunately no driver's education covering such situations.

Road Train – caution sign

The closer we came to the border with the Northern Territory, the worse the road conditions became. In a big state like Queensland, everything takes time, especially development, to reach all corners. The other reason could be the lack of cooperation between the States on a Federal level. The latter is a traditional problem indicating that people in Australia need more time to move towards a cohesive Federal identity.

CAMOOWEAL

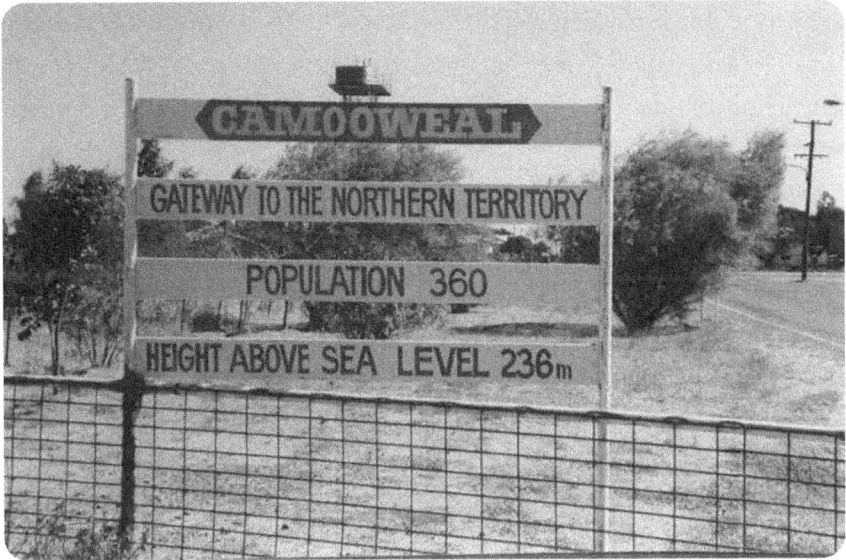

Camooweal welcome sign – N.W. Qld

Not far from the Northern Territory in dry, flat country, the hamlet of Camooweal turns up. In isolated places like this, the number of inhabitants and sometimes also a statement of the main activity in the place, like farming, cattle, mining, was often written under the name sign at the entrance to a town. On our arrival, Camooweal boasted 366 inhabitants. The main local establishments in a small place like this are the petrol station with the caravan park behind, a huge road train parking area next to it and the all-important pub.

No school could be seen from the short main road leading through the place. Probably School of the Air, a radio school was used here. The road was fairly wide, keeping the noise and dust from traffic away from the houses. Even though we had encountered very little traffic on our way, we found ourselves in a caravan park packed with visitors. There was only one site left for us to stay overnight, under an old Casuarina tree.

People holidaying here had the same vision we had on our return to Queensland from living in Hong Kong years before. "It is so rewarding to see so little for a change and to not have the view diminished in the way Hong Kong's sky-scrapers do." After setting up in the caravan park, on the other side of the fence, we saw Aborigines walking barefoot on the dusty road. They must have made up a high percentage of the local population. The youngsters were on the road playing with a ball and anything else they could get hold of. Clothes were not high on their agenda; a pair of shorts was usually enough; a t-shirt would be an added bonus.

Into that scene walked an elderly man in a tattered suit, trousers and jacket from different outfits, which unmistakably caught the eye. He also was walking barefoot, stiff as a stick on the dusty road with his curled grey hair flying in the evening breeze. His beard gave his whole face a serious, dignified expression. The youngsters on the road stopped their pranks when he passed; respect for age was still evident here. Appearance was not yet an issue. A dog also joined in the game of the young aboriginal boys. Its bark invited other dogs in the neighbourhood to join in.

With darkness setting into the place, the road next to the park turned silent again. No birds and no crickets farewelled the winter's day. During the night, the arrival of a road train on the other side of the park disrupted the silence, but not for long. The stars continued to send their light messages out of the dark sky well into the early morning hours, driven away only by a new day's sunrise.

The cold had gained the upper hand during the night, leaving the day to start with a brisk coolness. Our sleeping arrangements in the car allowed us a good night's sleep so that we could easily get up in the early twilight. A visit to look at the parked road trains revealed that they all came from the Northern Territory. One had cattle in all four trailers behind. The cows seemed to take their fate with a quiet 'moo' and their own personal odour. Empty trailers of other road trains were probably on the way further into Queensland, the drivers resting in comfort in the back of their well-equipped truck cabins.

As we were early, we left our car warming up outside the park. The lady on the petrol pump had this to say, after starting a yarn in order to bring a bit of life into the freezing cold of the morning, "Too many people are leaving the place; today the number of locals shown on the sign is much smaller. Our young people leave for the coast because they reckon there are more opportunities, and we can't get anybody to work on the pump or in the caravan park. One day only old people will live here; for now, one can just try to keep going."

Nobody will ever be spared problems; it is a fact of life. Sometimes we win and get the 'cream' but we can't have it all the time. The main thing always remains that we keep going by doing what we do best.

Disappearing bitumen before the Northern Territory

As we were only a short distance away from the Northern Territory, the road virtually disappeared into the bush after Camooweal. A diversion around a creek delivered an unwanted mud bath, changing our clean car into a dirty one. The dust that followed, stuck well to the mud on the outside. The powerful road trains had changed this into something having no resemblance to a road, making the remaining distance to the next State an adventure.

NORTHERN TERRITORY

On the State borderline, the road conditions changed markedly into uninterrupted bitumen road. The surface changed colour from pink to black and white, depending on the area where the fine stone used on the surface was collected. We were still in Australia, but with a difference; The Northern Territory is not a State but a Territory, ensuring it receives federal funding not state. The good condition of the roads was a testimony to the difference between State and Federal priorities.

In the future, when Federalism could work more effectively for all of Australia, Queensland might also have better roads. The small population, the good roads in the Northern Territory, and the lower traffic density meant that unlimited speed was allowed here. However, this required greater vigilance on the road.

BARKLY HOMESTEAD

The Barkly Tablelands extend to the north with distant hilly grasslands on both sides of the road. Communication towers near the road showed, in even distances of about 50 kilometres, where the road led. An umbrella-aerial on top of each tower directed frequencies to the next one, powered by solar units on the ground. On the roadside, a sign indicated which radio frequency could be received in the area. It was the only one; no other frequency was picked up. Mobile phones didn't work at all; transmitters were too far away to reach the outback. The telephone system worked though, where a phone was available.

We found ourselves mainly in cattle country with its huge properties. Along the way a branched road leading through a farm property indicated at its entrance the distance of 186 kilometres to a homestead. We had visited and described this homestead in 'Journey of a Lifetime' Volume 2. We didn't want to repeat the visit this time but it was a significant encounter with strong outback farmer-characters, an experience rarely found in today's world.

That was one farmer's life in the outback. Further west, we came upon another homestead on the Barkly Highway and decided to have a look at what he had done to succeed with the challenges here in the outback. The farmer balanced the struggle of cattle and wheat farming by inviting travellers onto his property to stay. He had established a luxurious stopover so that visitors were easily lured into staying.

Many had already taken up that invitation when we arrived at Barkly Homestead.

Barkley Homestead - Northern Territory

A fire-red bougainvillea in full bloom decorated the main building in front of a petrol station. Shopping facilities, restaurant, motel, and caravan park: everything was here in one spot, even a children's playground surrounded by fresh green cultivated lawn. All this was in the vast dry outback where the colour green was a rare sight, especially in the winter. A strong wind blew across the area; the temperature dropped all of a sudden so that we really felt it. Many visitors to the homestead didn't want to acknowledge the conditions, still wearing their shorts and t-shirts. They found out later how 'tough' they really were.

Our time at Barkley Homestead clearly showed us that climatic conditions could vary substantially at any time of the year in the outback. The homestead stood in a depression, where the cold air from the area moved in freely, as the strong cold winds blew. Not long after continuing on the Barkly Highway, it changed again into comfortably warm weather. Not even the pub or the pool table could persuade us to stay longer, as many others did, in this luxurious outback oasis. Everything depends on the goals of your journey, which naturally differ from person to person.

THE THREE WAYS

The Barkly Highway ended at the Three Ways, where it runs into the Stuart Highway, the main north-south arterial road in the Northern Territory. Recalling the trip from the border of Queensland to here, we realized that there were only two homesteads in the entire 450 kilometres, a tribute to the vastness of this outback area.

The Three Ways - Northern Territory

At the Three Ways we had two choices, either to go north to Darwin or south to Alice Springs. We decided on the latter. Because of the cold and rainy weather during that time of the year, coming from Adelaide in the south was an option, which we considered but rejected. On the other hand, coming from the north of the continent delivered a sunny, reliable, warm winter season.

TELEGRAPH STATION

Between the Three Ways and Tennant Creek we passed the old Telegraph Station with its restored stone buildings. The area had changed from flat country into rocky elevations, which indicated the higher central plateau of the continent. In the early days of telegraphic communication, South Australia had built a post here from which to explore further north into the continent. In 1871, the 3600 kilometres from Adelaide to Darwin were linked through telegraphic communication.

Telegraph Station – Northern Territory

In those early days, horses and camels were used to reach remote inland areas because there were no roads. The Telegraph Station quickly developed into a resting place that served as a supporting base as well. More stone buildings were erected. Today the place is well restored, and reflects an important part of outback history, when travelling in the area was a real challenge, and a contact through the Telegraph Station to the outer world was like a rescue mission. In those days, nothing was achieved easily in the outback.

TENNANT CREEK

We rolled into Tennant Creek one day earlier than originally intended. We were expecting the bus from Darwin to bring our daughter Gucki to meet us so that we could experience the Northern Territory together.

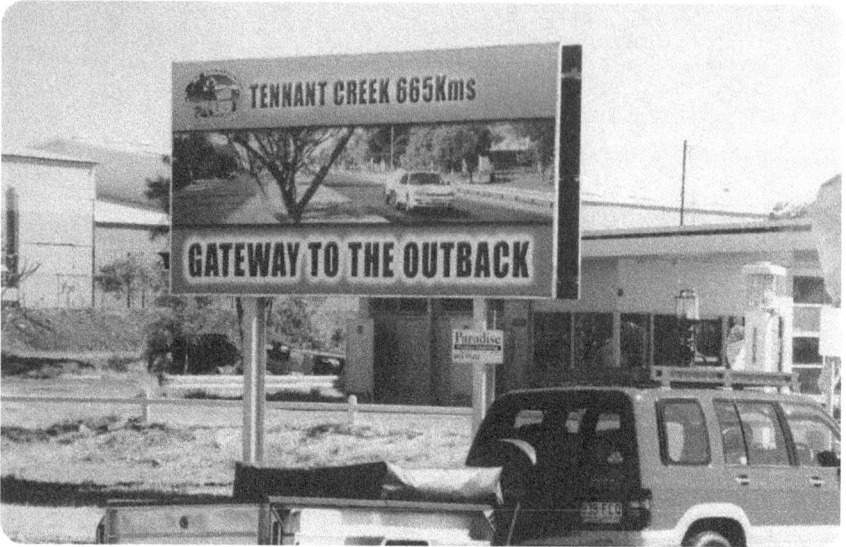

Tennant Creek - Northern Territory

A cold wind blew strongly from the south bringing heavy unseasonable cloud cover. The weather forecast had predicted a continued rain period around Ayers Rock. However, the clouds couldn't deliver any more rain, and most of it remained further south. A cold wind discouraged us from looking around the gold mining town and a place in the local caravan park became our preferred option. The park was already full with travellers from both interstate and overseas. Everybody was hoping the weather would change again to what it was supposed to be - predominantly sunshine.

The shopping facilities in Tennant Creek helped pass the time until the next morning, when the bus from Darwin was scheduled with our daughter on board. While waiting in front of the bus depot, a shop on the opposite side of the road piqued our curiosity with their sign 'Desert Dreams Hair Design'. I went across the road in an effort to fight off boredom only to find that the shop was closed. Its only drawcard for potential customers was a display of photos showing modern hairstyles. Would somebody with plenty of time up his sleeves come out of the bush for a haircut? It seemed strange.

Finally, the waiting was over as the bus arrived from Darwin. Our daughter Gucki was on it as agreed, carrying her backpack and also her guitar. She had left Darwin at 35 degrees Celsius and arrived in Tennant Creek where it was barely 5 degrees Celsius. Warm clothes became her first priority. As daytime advanced however, the weather started to improve again; the menacing clouds had moved out of the sky, and the wind died down, allowing the clear sunshine to warm everything up.

On the previous day, heavy bushfire smoke from burning scrub lay in the air. The local Aborigines considered it their traditional right to burn off land whenever they wanted to. In Australia, this burning for natural regeneration and consequent hunting of the trapped wildlife are complex issues. Just how much destruction is inflicted is not yet independently established. The limited burning of the past cannot establish a traditional right to burn today without any limits attached.

Nature's accidental selection helps to mobilize regeneration and selectively strengthen fauna and flora; systematic measures take away nature's accidental survival mechanism, destabilizing its existence with a result of a reduced recovery. The smoke still lay heavily over large black burnt regions, when we passed on our way further south. It was hard to believe that this burnt country could benefit anybody as everything was reduced to ashes.

A number of native plants benefit in their propagation from fire, because they originate from early times when the earth was still hot and frequently on fire because of wider volcanic activity or frequent lightning. The diversity of today's world supports all living forms in it and should not be addressed in a one-sided fashion like burning does. Nobody should try to turn the evolutionary clock back, because another evolution will never be the same.

The land going up to the Australian central plateau changed further south. Elevations ran across from east to west in equal distances of approximately 40 kilometres, looking like ancient moraines from previous ice ages. Where the bushfires had stopped, scattered bush with denser spots in some areas became visible along the sides of the road.

BARROW CREEK

We drove through Barrow Creek, a hamlet of only a couple of houses, which had made news with the murder case of a young British tourist. This terrible story really misrepresented the outback as a highly dangerous place.

The couple had parked their rented van near Barrow Creek on the side of the Stuart Highway for a night's rest. They were ambushed, the male companion disappearing and the young woman hiding just long enough in the surrounding bush to call for help at the nearby town. Such an incident was unprecedented in the outback. The couple had openly shown money about during camel-racing bets in Alice Springs, apparently to the wrong people, attracting attention and ensuring they were followed. Tourists cannot make the outback whatever they want. There will always be other elements of society who will inevitably mix with them.

We had no personal concerns about this incident, despite the media warning about the area. In the first place, we wouldn't let other people know what money we had and secondly we didn't stop overnight along a major arterial road without some kind of personal protection. All these insurances are good to have and it is even better when they are never needed.

THE DEVIL'S MARBLES

Further on, there was a field of huge rocks in the middle of flat land close to the road. These were the famous Devil's Marbles. Over time erosion had exposed these huge rock formations. The name indicates that only a 'Devil' could have moved them. Their shapes are mostly rounded off through nature's erosion resulting in a few single outstanding spherical boulders of gigantic dimensions.

Our first sight of the Devil's Marbles – Northern Territory

Up close to the Devil's Marbles

The Devil's Marbles - Central Australia, Northern Territory.

We appeared insignificant in front of them. The boulders are of a hard rock conglomerate of various colours - grey, black, white and red. To discourage visitors from taking samples, it is said, "The 'Devil' will be with you, if you own his rock."

In places, where innumerable rock fragments could be found, we dared to take one small 'Devil' with us, which hasn't so far turned out to be a bad 'Devil'. We have a hobby of collecting stones from around the world, which makes us 'stone-rich' if nothing else!

The largest of the Marbles

The further south we travelled, the less warmth the sun produced during the day. A crystal-clear winter sky gained the upper hand after an unseasonable two weeks of rain. The positive side to the rain was that the bush looked fresh and green and started to flower earlier, transforming the entire area into an unexpected spring enchantment.

Dense bush on a hillside attracted our attention. I stopped off the road, wanting to catch the colourful impression of the dark-red soil with its scattered colourful mineral rocks everywhere and the dark green bush with its yellow wattle flowers in between. A wire fence parallel to the road stopped me going further.

Tropic of Capricorn – Northern Territory

Just then, another vehicle arrived, stopping next to us. A couple with their daughter emerged asking first in broken English, "What is here to take photos from? We come from Germany and would like to learn more about Australia." My German answer took them by surprise. "How is it possible that you talk fluently German to us and tell us that you are an Australian?"

"This is Australia where people come from all parts of the world, speaking English in public but at home often speaking their mother-tongue like we do. In our case, we don't speak only German at home, but also Finnish, because my wife comes from Finland."

"This is incredible; we haven't heard it before. Can you show us, what sparked your interest in the area?"

"Just look at the vast land around with its abundance of colours - no human beings except us, no town for a long distance; this is something you won't find in Germany. Look at the sun in that crystal azure blue sky. You can't see this any more in most places on earth."

"How did you come to Australia? Did you come with your family?"

As I answered their questions, I let them know that visiting Australia is one thing, but receiving permanent residence is another much more complex issue. A move to Australia involves determination and constant effort to adjust to Australian conditions. These conditions are not easily recognised from a tourist point of view. This encounter of our two families had to be limited, as we wanted to reach Alice Springs during daylight and not have to spend the night in the bush.

What surprised us in this and other meetings, was the light-heartedness of foreigners travelling here in the outback, as if this were somewhere in Germany. Money can do a lot, but should not excuse people from being careful. The Australian outback is very different from Europe and begs for caution, especially when travelling on your own. Any problem in this environment can become very much your problem, requiring you also, in many cases, to tackle it on your own. Help is always welcome here in the outback but one should not count on it. Self is the man!

Another note is probably worth mentioning here. Taking pets with you into the outback creates a problem in many places like wild animal sanctuaries, National Parks, and natural sights of interest where pets generally are barred from entering. For this reason we had left our German Shepherds at home to keep their vigil during our absence and watch over our son Micki.

ALICE SPRINGS

Alice Springs – Northern Territory

The Northern Territory's second largest city announced itself atop a big roof-shaped bush rock in letters - Alice Springs. The road descended from here to the plain in front of the MacDonnell Ranges, which block the land from east to west. This rugged, rocky mountain range stood wild out of the land; no forests could take a foothold on the steep slopes. Pockets of bush covered the lower areas. Houses down on the plain were spreading in numbers but stood well off the MacDonnell Ranges.

As soon as the road reached the outskirts of Alice Springs, avenues of old growth acacias lined both sides of the main road, closing in the sky with their leaf canopies. The city reflects a magic beauty through its natural sceneries. It is true that 'there is no other town like Alice'.

When looking at the number of foreign tourists trying to catch a glimpse of a major outback town, it seemed the locals were in a minority. Aborigines made up the other principal part of the town's population. They are living more by themselves and do not like to be addressed with curiosity. Their understanding of life is different from our western society. We should learn to watch first and gain impressions this way. The best time to communicate with them is when they move towards you.

Throughout history Aborigines have become suspicious of white Australians. Only ones who can break down such barriers with distance, time and patience, will gain their trust back.

Some years later I met a teacher from Hermannsburg, which is located in the middle of the MacDonnell Ranges. He passed on this information. "After years with Aborigines I started to understand them even less and less. Just when you think you have learnt something about them, they set you back on a learning curve. They seem to have a much more complex understanding than we usually develop. Their teacher has always been nature; if we want to live along side them, we have to connect to them through their understanding of nature.

When interacting, the indigenous Australian always seems to connect with questions from their own understanding - if they are encouraged to do so. They want to be heard and not just told. The real problems start in our society when Aborigines become largely isolated from their traditional ways and become insecure when they don't belong any more to either society. Often they then become primed for radical ideas, which don't originate from their traditional understanding but become a vehicle for other ideas. A two-way education with mutual respect is the answer to integrate Aborigines successfully into a modern society. Let them maintain their part of an understanding for the benefit of all."

The caravan park in Alice Springs couldn't be missed. It was well laid out to accommodate many visitors. As soon as the sun disappeared, incredible cold moved into the place dropping the temperature during the night to minus eight degrees Celsius. This became too much to bear for our daughter Gucki, who fell very sick, forcing us to send her back with the next bus to the 35 degrees Celsius of Darwin. Despite our best intentions, our plan to experience the Northern Territory together fell apart.

My wife and I didn't come so far however to abandon the tour. As the next day again recovered from this cold snap, our journey continued as planned. Before leaving Alice Springs for Ayers Rock, we walked on foot through the city mall. Its modern shops and landscaped gardens surprised everybody, making you forget that you were in the semi-desert. The stranded father and son from Longreach crossed our path here with a big hallo. Their car problem was long forgotten. It was good to meet them again, if only in passing. After shopping in a modern supermarket, our interest focussed away from this town towards the south, past the MacDonnell Ranges.

THE TODD RIVER

The Todd River had broken a passage in the southeast corner of Alice Springs, allowing the river and the road to pass closely. Unseasonable rain over the past two weeks had delivered some water to the riverbed. Boat racing in the Todd River usually takes place during springtime, when the river is dry. Yes, you are reading correctly - the Todd River boat race is an event taking place in the river when it has no water, which would be the case most of the time through the year.

Todd River

As the river carried water, the race had to be postponed until the river was dry again.

Typical outback humour accompanies the race where the competing teams lift their boats out of the dry sandy riverbed, stand inside the boat without a floor, and run the distance on foot. This event draws big crowds from the area, but also from other parts of the continent, including the ever-present overseas tourists. Bets, beer, and barbecues under a clear outback sunny sky guarantee lots of fun. Having no water in the Todd River doesn't stop the outback communities having their own special kind of fun.

Visitors to the area contribute greatly to the economy of this outback area, where they can experience the immense open spaces of the outback and its own special natural beauties. The land past the passage of the Todd River turned green and there was cultivated farming land for a short distance, returning to dry outback bushland soon after. Leaving the MacDonnell Ranges behind, the land continued flat to the horizon.

AYERS ROCK

At Erldunda we left the Stuart Highway and went west on a pilgrimage to the largest monolith on earth: Ayers Rock, called Uluru by the Aborigines. Before the intersection, a big modern centre serviced travellers on their tour through the outback. Loaded buses with passengers mainly from Adelaide in the south and private vehicles created some traffic during certain times of the day. As we carried on, we had to keep an eye on the time in order to reach Ayers Rock before darkness. Everybody else must have left for Uluru or arrived from it earlier, because we met no traffic on our way at all.

The bitumen road remained fairly good on this last leg of 240 kilometres. Only two evenly distanced roadhouses lay between Erldunda and the Rock. Scattered bush reflected in its fresh green the beginning of light blossom colours. Red soil and bush rocks (as if somebody had left them behind) were everywhere. The bush was fairly low, resisting the harsh weather conditions of strong winds, cold winter nights, long dry spells, sometimes floods, and of course the extreme heat during summer.

Uluru - Ayers Rock - from 40kms away

Uluru – coming closer

While driving, our eyes looked further west trying to catch the moment when Uluru appeared on the horizon. And suddenly there it was, 140 kilometres away, a long stretched silhouette rising out of the endless plain that led towards it. From the distance, Uluru seemed to disappear on the long-bowed horizon. Its colours were grey-green. Every kilometre that we came closer, it rose further up out of the ground, starting to change colours. We arrived during daylight outside the rock area in the satellite town of Yulara.

Tourists in their thousands could choose here from hotel accommodation of extreme luxury, if you were prepared to pay for it, to a large area of caravan and camping grounds, where most of the natural bush was left in place. Before finding accommodation, we moved on and paid Uluru our first visit. On the way was a checkpoint, where an entrance fee was charged and where all visitors were informed that they had to be out of the Uluru - Kata Tjuta National Park by 7.30 p.m. Staying overnight in the park was not allowed.

What caught my attention was that this was sacred Aboriginal territory, where a small community of Aboriginals were permanent residents, claiming Uluru as their property and charging visitors a respectable entrance fee. None of the personnel in the park however was Aboriginal. Are we doing the right thing on behalf of them? If they are the declared owners, shouldn't they also look after their own affairs or at least participate? Holding Aborigines 'in tutelage' is not a good move; they need eventually to learn to manage their own affairs. To leave them sitting on the side and present them as quasi 'exhibition pieces' in a cultural centre demeans the necessary ongoing dialogue on all levels. There is still a long way to go to reach mutual understanding and acceptance of Aborigines.

In front of the monolith a circuit drive leads eastwards to a parking area right in front of the steep rising rock wall. The sun was already setting behind the horizon, covering Ayers Rock entirely in colour, ranging from light to dark red and changing over into dark blue. The rock giant governs here over complete silence. One wonder of the world left us enchanted at the end of the day.

Next morning another day invited us to visit Ayers Rock. In the parking area at the foot of the rock there were other visitors. Just as we prepared to start our visit, a German film producer with two attractive female models approached us, asking us a number of questions, which we couldn't answer properly as we had only just arrived ourselves. Later we learnt that in some areas along the rock, signs prohibited the taking of photos out of respect for this sacred Aboriginal site. There were even substantial fines for a breach of this request. The German gentleman was visibly upset.

"I come all the way from Germany with my two models and can't take the photos I want. Nobody tells you this before you arrive here. This is different from America; you can take any photos wherever you want."

The reason photos are not permitted in parts of Uluru is that what is sacred for the Aborigines should not be exploited commercially, particularly posing models (no matter how beautiful), which this film producer had in mind. Fortunately, Australia is still different from America!

At least we had received first information from the area and decided to have a look for ourselves the next day. When passing the checkpoint of the park, the darkness of the night took over quickly. Ayers Rock became visible only as a dark colossus against the sky with its rising moon and innumerable stars. Even the bush lay dark and silent in the vast flat land. The cold of the winter night moved in unstoppably, urging us to find a place in the caravan park to stay for the night.

Under the cover of casuarinas we could still find a not too crowded place. Next morning we sought the first sunshine as early as possible to shake off the night's cold. Our day's destination became Uluru (Ayers Rock) and Kata-Tjuta (the Olgas). Again we had to pass through the park's checkpoint to look at Uluru. It was the only way for us to pay our visit to the monolith. Luckily, the ban on climbing Ayers Rock had just been suspended after two weeks of mourning an Aboriginal elder.

My wife Arja on the Uluru walk

Uluru - rock detail

From the Mala car park, a chain anchored on posts in regular distances assisted with the first part of a climb on the steep rock wall. Clear sunshine spanned the sky and conditions were ideal for a climb. A lot of people also wanted to go up, but many didn't reach the first goal, where the chain ended. Initially, my wife became a bit uncertain watching others when they stopped moving. A focus away from these others strengthened her so that we could support each other and arrive convincingly past the first hurdle.

Looking down and across the land well and truly compensated for the effort involved. Our car was still visible; bush laid a green carpet over the land and there was a road visible, cutting in a straight thin line through it. Far away on the northern horizon the dark band of the MacDonnell Ranges could be seen, where Alice Springs lay behind. A pile of huge rounded boulders was visible, mountain-like not far in the distance to the west. These were Kata-Tjuta (the Olgas). Directly around us the plane rock-surfaces pointed in steps and elevations towards the summit.

The steep ascent behind us, the path led further towards the monolith's central area, giving more and more views in other directions. The rock continued in renewed grand steps falling away towards the flat land underneath. Further up the rock, the area became more of a crosswalk to the centre's highest point of 867 metres. Recent rain had filled the rock pools along the way, providing an excellent source of drinking water. Closer to the summit a stiff wind reached us from the south, blowing cold air.

A plaque on top of a stone marked Ayer's Rock summit. Both my wife and myself made the climb and felt proud of it, as our encounter had included the highly spiritual aspect of the trek, and reflected the esteem that its Aboriginal population holds for Uluru. Nobody else was with us on the summit. We took the imposing views with us as a sacred treasure, which is how Aborigines want us to understand their Uluru. All around bowed the horizon giving the strong impression that we were here atop of the world: grassland, bush, rocky fields changed in colours from yellow-brown, green to reddish. Only the sky above us seemed to match the endless view to the earth.

Uluru summit with the Olgas in the background

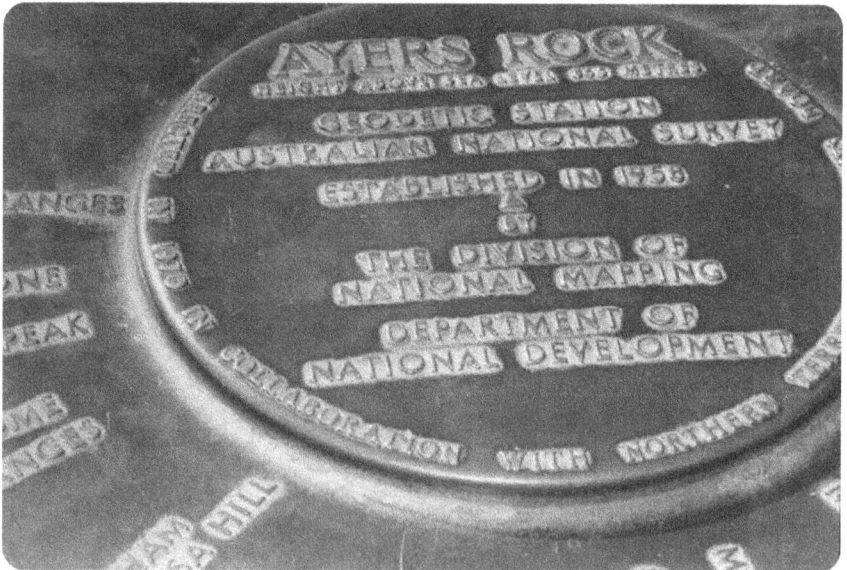

Uluru summit post

In the far southeast another monolith was visible, marginally smaller than Ayers Rock. No humans, no houses, no cars could be seen from the top; we had shrunk to insignificance 'in front of nature's altar to the universe' in this ancient centre of Australia.

What does the term monolith mean? Ayers Rock is the largest monolith on earth; its composition is one piece of rock, which counts for the name monolith (mono meaning one). It is composed of sandstone stratification. Due to this sediment sandstone, it can be inferred that Ayers Rock continues underground. Ice ages must have carried away covering layers of the monolith, which were eventually found in the east-west ranges in regular distances on our way to the south of the Northern Territory. Such a huge shift in earth masses reminds us of the geological age of this continent, not matched elsewhere. The age of the Australian continent is a strong element in the Aboriginal association with nature. We are bound to respect nature's oldest work of art.

Returning to the base of Ayers Rock didn't require any more effort than going up, which is not the case in all such descents. When arriving from a crosswalk at the edge of the rock wall, the fixed chain assisted with the rest of the descent, where the land underneath came in sight and our parked car appeared like a small pinhead in the vast plain.

Back on the footsteps of the monolith, we undertook a walk through a small eucalypt forest and bush into Kamtju Gorge. Recent rain had brought back to the bush new shoots and leaves of vivid colours. There was the beginning of a rich carpet of flowers. In the Gorge still water lay across a footpath. The water had come down mainly vertical rock walls marked with furrows over a long time and running side by side up to the top edge. Time had marked the monolith differently in many places, giving rise to the many stories of the Aborigines, in which they explained their understanding of nature.

A typical Aboriginal story about Uluru can be found in "Australian Legends and Landscapes" by Oodgeroo Noonuccal. There are many Aboriginal stories of interest in this source.

THE MUTITJULU STORY

Mutitjulu is the community name for the Pitjantjatjara people living at Uluru. Kapi Mutitjulu is the only reliable waterhole at Uluru, and has been used by the Pitjantjatjara people for thousands of years. All of the features in the Mutitjulu area are associated with the creation history of a group of closely connected ancestral beings, the most important of which are two snakes, Kuniya and Liru (western brown-snake). Wherever you walk in this area, you are surrounded by the presence of Kuniya and Liru Tjukurrpa.

In the beginning, the female Kuniya becomes very angry after being publicly insulted by her nephew, Liru. She attacks him in a great rage, and the battle becomes a disastrous encounter. As Kuniya approaches Liru in her righteous anger, she performs a ritual dance to make it publicly known that a woman of power is seeking to punish the person who has insulted her. Kuniya is furious, and in an attempt to control the dark forces that her ritual anger is unleashing, she picks up a handful of sand and lets it fall to the ground. This is to settle the forces she is disturbing, so that they will not harm others.

However, Kuniya's rage is too strong, and a great battle takes place. Kuniya strikes Liru and he receives a small wound as he deflects the blow with his shield. Then Kuniya strikes Liru a second time and he receives a deep, long and fatal wound. Liru's shield falls with him to the ground. Kuniya has avenged her honour, but because of her furious rage every plant near the battlefield has become poisoned. Evidence of Kuniya's actions as she rushes towards her insulter and destroys him, is clear in the features of Uluru, and is celebrated today in story, song and ritual dance.

The quintessence of the story is: 'Who is in a furious rage, only spreads his poison!'

Warayukio and Ngaltawata are points along the monolith declared sacred, because they translate images out of our lives in nature, like birth, that are not allowed to be documented. A sacred shrine requires a personal pilgrimage and cannot be spoken about nor replaced by images. This is an ancient belief, which we have to learn to respect.

We should also never forget that everybody has something sacred in his or her life, usually beginning where knowledge stops and beliefs begin. On one of the upper rock faces appears the 'Brain', a surface disintegration on a large scale showing a brain-shape in the contour of a skull. Is this the brain of the monolith? Long shades from Ayers Rock indicated daylight was disappearing again, making room for the night's darkness and devouring all the shade quickly. Returning to our campsite in Yulara, Ayers Rock stood behind us, now blacker than the night after having displayed its colourful changes.

Uluru – 'The Brain' formation

Uluru's 'The Brain' up close

The 29th of July marked a special day in our personal calendar; 36 years earlier, my wife and I met for the first time on that date in Stockholm, Sweden. An excellent restaurant in the area gave us the opportunity to celebrate this anniversary in style. It was particularly special, because in the wilderness of central Australia we could enjoy luxury too, a contrast that only served to highlight the occasion for us. Even a local wine named 'Red Centre' was offered. The service however was very slow and, when talking to the waitresses, we learnt that the restaurant was desperately short of staff. Every guest therefore was offered a well-paid job in exchange for an extended holiday. People on holiday obviously hadn't responded favourably. Despite the number of visitors, the atmosphere remained silent. The grandness of Australia's Centre humbled visitors as they paid due respect to its grandeur.

KATA TJUTA – THE OLGAS

After another cold night, it was decided to pay a visit to Kata Tjuta (the Olgas), located west of Uluru. The road leading through dense bushland stopped in front of another of nature's spectacle; an accumulation of massive monoliths stood rising out of the plain, never quite reaching the height of Ayers Rock. The completely round contours of these monoliths also reflected the ancient earth's history. Having been shaped through time by nature's elements: wind, water, drought, heat, cold and most likely ice ages, they now stood silently alone.

The Olgas

The road stopped at a parking area, where only a footpath continued another short distance to a slightly elevated platform. Visitors gained a panoramic view of Kata-Tjuta and the land around. A fence stopped people from going further, because the land in front of the Olgas houses a grove of ancient Desert Oaks. The age of these oaks can only be estimated. This is the only place on earth that they grow. The grove is a living fossil museum.

Desert oaks - The Olgas

In these dry, extreme climatic conditions everything grows so slowly that their growth could not be estimated over one short human life span. The tree trunks were black from grassfires; their canopies displayed long, hanging, fresh green needles of about five centimetres in length. Is this tree a relative of the Casuarina tree, which has similar needles, but different bark? Which tree is older and has moved across evolution's history? Has the Desert Oak remained here in isolation? The two types of tree have common ancient characteristics: drought, fire, water resistant and even salt-water tolerant. This indicates that they have survived times of inundation by seawater, just like Mangroves and Boab trees.

It was good to see that the fragile environment of the Desert Oaks enjoyed complete protection from human interference. Even walking on the sandy soil of this nature's grove could compact it, so that the moisture from the night's dew would run off and reduce the sensitive lifeline of a tree, which was most likely established over millions of years ago. Yellow, dry grass stood between the trees, each single straw separate from each other and looking like grassland.

The reddish monolith colossus behind created an impression of its own; it is not desert, not lush, but grand, elemental, colourful and therefore unique, found only in Australia's Centre. A naturalist, an artist, a scientist, and a photographer - they can all experience nature's Mecca here, but they must go in search.

Halfway back to Yulara we found the Cultural Aboriginal Centre. Labyrinth-like passages led through a number of close-by huts, which exhibited typical Aboriginal artwork, using displays and video to tell visitors about the land and its meaning to Aborigines. The striking aspect of the Centre was once more that no Aborigine could be seen. In front of this display I asked myself, do the owners agree on everything that is expressed here? Why don't they take part in this demonstration? Was this a display of how we want the Aborigines to be understood?

Aborigines express a superb simplicity through their art in their direct dialogue with nature. Coloured points arranged into symbolic creatures on a plain-coloured background was evidence of the Aboriginal art expression, referring to the multiple fragile building blocks of everything in nature. A representation in regular patterns of a snake, a kangaroo, fish, mountain ranges, a river, rocks and the sun is how Aborigines see their role in nature, all in superb simplicity of expression of their culture.

We on the other hand have become far too complex to go back and live on an elementary basis in nature. Our progress and drive make a return to nature's origins difficult, if not impossible. The small numbers of indigenous Aborigines most often live today in Aboriginal Land Trusts, where non-Aborigines need State permission for a limited visit. This raises certain questions.

Mistakes of the past have led to strict regulations, for instance to prohibit bringing alcohol onto a Land Trust. Efforts are made to help Aborigines in many ways in their traditional environment with housing, health care, and education. Could what has been handled wrongly in the past continue to be handled wrongly today? Supplying services to Aborigines is one thing, but making them dependant this way is another issue. Can we motivate Aborigines to come forward with their own efforts so that they can slowly integrate into our society?

A lot of detailed groundwork has still to be done in order to allow other Aboriginal elements of society to merge with our society; otherwise such a process will remain futile. In 2007, police and army were sent into Aboriginal communities to establish 'order', showing only how much we have failed in that task. Misunderstandings are the most common result of unbalanced measures. A small part of the Aboriginal community receives free school transport, health care, school materials, uniforms, luncheons; this naturally upsets some white Australians who have to provide everything themselves.

Even with the best intentions on both sides, a process of 'reconciliation' will take time. A better understanding of indigenous Australians will pave the path towards coexistence and not to a separate life. Even if we could meet halfway, the problem would still be with us - how to get along with Aborigines. In this difficult process, we see groups of Aborigines who live closer to us in cities becoming all too often disappointed with the progress they see, which they were rightly or wrongly led to believe would solve their problems. We shouldn't all become misled and believe that money will fix all the problems. Only continued effort along with the support of money will bring long -term solutions.

MACDONNELL RANGES

Time told us to move on from Uluru. A long drive to Darwin in the Top End of the Northern Territory lay in front of us. Instead of going back to Alice Springs on the same bitumen road, halfway to the Stuart Highway we took instead a stony branched-off dusty road north into the mighty MacDonnell Ranges. A four-wheel drive is highly recommended for this leg of the trip and also some off-road experience. This part of the 'Centre' is so impressive that visitors can feel as though they have been moved to another planet exhibiting unexpected beauty. Driving alone and leaving dust clouds behind in the air offers 'compensation' for the efforts required during this part of the tour. Our first stop was King's Canyon.

KING'S CANYON

King's Canyon is a mighty cleft in the George Gill Range. Situated 325 kilometres west of Alice Springs, the massive walls of the Canyon tower over rock water pools and lush vegetation. The sandstone walls rise up to 300 metres and are spotted with abstract rock patterns carved by wind and water. From the top of the Canyon a spectacular view includes the 'Lost City' and the valley known as 'the Garden of Eden'. When the sun changes its position in the sky, the colours do the same in the rock walls, moving from yellow to dark red along with all the nuances between.

King's Canyon

HERMANNSBURG

After King's Canyon, a permit is required to access Mereenie Hoop Road, which continues eastwards to Hermannsburg, an Aboriginal settlement. For a foreign tourist, it is difficult and time consuming to get a permit unless one has solid reasons for wanting to tour the area. Hermannsburg is a typical remote Aboriginal community with an infrastructure of housing assistance, education, and health care, delivered by the Government. Only the future will tell how successful such help/dependence has become.

When Aborigines are taught to step in and take joint responsibility for their own affairs along with Government officials, then a future of common goals is more likely to be achieved. Looking at the Aboriginal community at Hermannsburg, indicates that there is still a lot to be done to maintain what has been achieved and give the Aboriginal community free hand in their own decision making; the place is still a far cry from an urban community. Only time and patience will succeed, where two different worlds want to meet.

Aboriginal land north of Hermannsburg can be accessed only from Alice Springs. This area is where Mount Sonder is located: one of the Centre's giants, rising to a height of 1330 metres. The rock from which it is formed is estimated to be 400 million years old. Also west of Alice Springs in the Jay Creek Aboriginal Reserve, the awesome Stanley Chasm splits the MacDonnell Ranges. Here, cliffs standing 60 to 75 metres high and only four to five metres apart, change colour dramatically as the sun strikes the deep recesses. The Chasm is named after Mrs. Ida Standley, the first schoolteacher in Alice Springs.

Mount Sonder - Macdonnell Ranges, Northern Territory

Stanley Chasm - Macdonnell Ranges

NORTHBOUND TO THE TOP END

After returning to Alice Springs, we continued our journey north. Along the road a completely fenced-off property became visible in the west, something not commonly seen in the outback. What caught our attention even more than the perfect fence work was the green fruit tree plantation behind. Outside this large fenced area, the Australian bush struggled to survive in the midst of rock material and hardly any useful soil; whereas inside the fenced area grew pears, peaches, apples, oranges, lemons and grapevines in a straight line on perfectly evenly distanced espaliers, looking so healthy and green, as if inside the fenced area a different world had started.

Rocks were used to border garden beds, which contained visibly cultivated dark-red topsoil, while passages laid with stone ran between the beds. Here was the home of the 'Red Centre' wine. Water for the irrigation had been tapped from an artesian well and behind the whole enterprise there was one family, which had migrated from Zimbabwe, formerly Rhodesia, in southern Africa. It was amazing to see what human determination can create: a regular Garden of Eden in a desert environment.

Outback Camel Station – Northern Territory

Not far from this unparalleled horticultural farm, a Camel Farm was established on the western side of the highway surrounded by green meadows. A big sign invited:

'Welcome to Camel Outback Safaris', which included onsite farmhouse accommodation and hospitality. The place looked well established from the road, from where the camel paddocks sent a penetrating scent into the air. Another Zimbabwean family had settled here in this difficult environment and succeeded in turning poor looking land into an oasis. A pet African ostrich had its own paddock, indicating that it also had adapted well to the Australian conditions.

Much of the African wildlife can also live here in Australia, as is the case near the New South Wales town of Dubbo. Here, a huge sanctuary for African wildlife has been successfully established with the noble idea of helping to save some of the wildlife that is left in today's world. Australia can offer similar conditions to Africa and has the space to create sanctuaries for endangered species like the Black Rhino. Visitors to the Dubbo Wildlife Park in the southeast of the continent will be surprised to be able to undertake safaris with lions, giraffes, antelopes and elephants right here in Australia.

People in Australia could be considered as having the heart to care for endangered animals. This is also shown in the country's legislation and signs for the protection of all animals: a snake on the road has to be respected by traffic and not be run over. However accidents can, and often do, happen when a car gives way to something on the road. It can collide with something else instead. Negligence towards wildlife is subjected to penalties. On the other hand it is difficult to control and therefore many dead kangaroos can be found on roads outside populated areas. The law is in place, but the arm is not long enough to reach out everywhere.

Camels from the Outback are renown for their excellent breeding stock and sold mainly to Arabian countries, back to their more traditional origins. One determined migrant has made this possible in Australia. The odour from the camel paddocks didn't reach the farmhouse, because it was protected from the prevailing wind, so that visitors could be invited to stay in the shaded farmhouse complex under a group of big fig trees. The camel farmer's family had made good contacts with the local Aboriginal communities, inviting them to exhibit their artwork on the property so that guests could purchase them: where there's a will, there's a way! As we had no camel safari on our minds, the road to the north became our priority before the end of the day.

Camels at rest

TI TREE

We reached Ti Tree along the Stuart Highway in the Ahakeye Aboriginal Land Trust before dusk. A petrol station with a caravan park behind was all you could see. As we learned next morning, the Aborigines living in the community further inland showed up only occasionally.

Ti Tree caravan park entrance

Ti Tree – Northern Territory

Our attention focussed first on the caravan park, which was well established, and where a row of cotton palms on both sides of a driveway led away from the road. A windmill on the roadside pumped water from underground into high aboveground raised tanks supplying the water to the park facilities. The orange grove in the back became the perfect place for us to stay overnight. Only a few other travellers joined us in the large fenced-off park area.

At the entrance, a paddock held a number of kangaroos and one emu, giving a good opportunity for visitors to watch them up close. The kangaroos hopped around inside the fenced paddock, whereas the emu walked stubbornly along only one side of the fence, up and down, and did not become distracted at all from outside, looking as if it was thinking hard about something.

Ti Tree - historic wagon

An old wagon left on the side of the paddock told a story of bygone pioneering days and had also found its place of rest here. Nothing is thrown away or has a use-by-date in the outback. The night's chill made us seek the cosiness of a bed inside our car. During the night here, it remained dead silent under a clear, southern starry sky; no other light took away this enchanting shine.

Next morning we took our time to get petrol at the station near the highway. Life did not start here until the cold of the night had given way to a new day's sunshine. Initially we were alone at the petrol station, but soon after, eight Aboriginal children headed by two teenaged girls, arrived on the scene, looking curiously at our car. Our introduction to them was, "Would you like to be in a photo?"

At first there was no response, so I continued, "An ice-cream - will that be okay as payment for taking a photo with all of you in it?" As an answer, the kids led the way to the shop to find the ice cream. While I paid the petrol and ice cream bill, the kids waited outside, armed with a sweet of their choice. The photo could now go ahead, not much further explanation was required. As I prepared my camera for the snapshot, I asked them to come closer together for the photo. Just when I pressed the camera button, all the kids showed a gesture of disdain with their raised fingers, which I must admit surprised me immensely.

These Aboriginal kids were already brought up with a deeply rooted criticism of white Australians; how wrong was I to ask them for a photo with a treat as 'payment'? The different situation between them and us possibly triggered this free expression indicating that there was also a different understanding between the two sides. The photo taken, the kids took off as they had arrived, no further comments left behind. Our tour continued through familiar territory, which somehow looked different because we were travelling in the opposite direction.

TENNANT CREEK

Arriving again in Tennant Creek, the local supermarket got our custom once more. Aborigines from the nearby Land Trust, Warumungu were in front of us at the cash register - adults and teenaged children, probably ten all together. The service had come to a halt, nothing moved for quite a while until it became evident that the lady at the cash register waited for the money for the goods the kids had taken in the shop. One Aboriginal woman with the kids called for the men, who had already slipped by the counter.

She turned out the trouser pockets of one man after the other, failing to collect any money to finalize the bill. The kids meanwhile got stuck into their coke, ice cream, chocolate and biscuits beyond the point of return and proudly showing their acquisitions. All this had possibly started at home; kids often like pestering parents at great length for a shopping spree, until the parents give in. Now came the bill and with it the reality that the money was not quite enough.

The lady at the register insisted on the full amount paid. As time went on and no sign of a solution turned up, I went to the cashier asking her how much was owed on the bill; it was exactly fifty cents. As I asked the Aboriginal woman whether she had any objection to my helping out, she was all smiles, telling the kids to move and join the others outside. The queue behind could move on again now.

Once we had also passed through the cash register, we moved outside to our car. After leaving the shop, all the Aboriginal adults stood in front of the exit in one place, no kids with them. I tried to farewell them with a friendly hand sign, while they remained totally motionless, looking at my wife and me and saying nothing at all. Here we were again; who could have interpreted this whole situation reliably? Are we miles apart in our understanding with Aborigines? I am not too sure about that, a bit like the teacher from Hermannsburg.

Meeting Aborigines was best in the Northern Territory, where they lived more traditionally than in other parts of Australia. In the semi-desert centre of Australia, Aborigines can be found to differ from their people in the north, at the Top End. Food here is limited to tough kangaroo meat, witchetty grubs and a few underground roots. In the tropics of the Top End, fish was always available in rivers, billabongs and on the seaside. This dietary difference had a profound impact on their appearance.

The tough inland living conditions made the Aborigines slim and rather tall, whereas their counterparts in the north seemed to be more solid, because of different proteins and minerals mainly from the fish in their diets. Changing their long established traditional diet for the purpose of helping them is not necessarily a good idea. This is also evident in some Pacific Islanders; when civilisation changes a traditional diet, people quickly put on weight, because their body can't break down the 'foreign food'.

At a petrol station along Stuart Highway in the middle of nowhere, an Aborigine cross-legged on the green grass. How long he had been in this place watching things happening and how old he was, nobody could really tell.

Indigenous elder on roadside

The green of the irrigated grass became attractive enough for him to spend some part of his day there; in the nearby Land Trust there was no such green area during winter. Was he happy, depressed, or just waiting for something? No such emotion could be seen either in his idle position or in his face, which the long, grey, disorderly hair partly concealed. Resorting to the warm sunshine was another likely motive, as he carried nothing along with him. To enter into an exchange of words could have upset the man in his quiet observations; our language was not his, which eventually opens a further gap in the understanding between us.

One thing was sure, he was not in a hurry and had all the time on his side watching the occasional traveller enter the petrol station and take off soon after. Was he thinking, "Why are people on the move? I don't have to move. I am happy where nature has left me." Who was right or wrong now? The future might tell him one day that we both were right but in different ways.

I find such observations important, because indigenous people express themselves more than we do with hardly visible sign language reflecting on their natural caution, which doesn't relate much to words. The descendants of the Incas in remote parts of Chile, Peru and Ecuador appeared to us in a similar way. Not only the language separates people from each other, but also a deep historical consciousness often plays a vital role. Too frequently in the past we had succeeded in enforcing our culture on other people, not realising what the other side in such a process has given up and lost, not only for them, but also for all of us. Dealing effectively with Australia's Aborigines is a very sensitive issue, which can never be addressed with one-sided views.

Closer to Tennant Creek, bush fires were still raging on both sides of the road, sending heavy smoke clouds high up and obscuring the sun even during daylight. Wedge-tailed eagles circled in the air, where the fire had passed, looking for 'grilled lizards' and anything else that couldn't escape the savaging fire. As soon as we dropped our speed, these huge birds of prey took off, but remained in one spot as long as the speed was kept up, knowing a fast car will not stop and possibly be a danger to them.

We had already experienced this previously in other parts of Australia. As I wanted to take a photo of a wedge-tailed eagle, which sat on a dead kangaroo on the side of the road, we slowed down. Suddenly a truck arrived from behind, forcing me to speed up again and abandon the photo opportunity; the eagle on the other hand watched this while not moving at all from the scene.

Past the Three Ways, where we arrived earlier from Queensland in the east, tea-trees with their dark green bushy needles became one of the dominant types of vegetation. The temperature started to pick up the further north we came. Tea-trees have an intense scent; its needles can be used either for tea or oil, which when extracted makes an excellent disinfectant.

Eucalypt trees showed up, scattered and in small pockets, supplying also disinfectants through their leaves and trunks as well. Over 200 Eucalypt species call Australia home, representing the primary stock of all eucalypt trees in the world. All native trees of Australia are eucalypts; they are very dominant and their roots are known to reach any depth in the ground for water. One healthy eucalypt tree circulates 200 litres of water through its system every day.

How tough 'Aussies' are. Reafforestation efforts in northern Spain have shown with Australian eucalypts that the eucalypts killed all the other vegetation around and established itself with superiority. Spain had an even bigger problem when trying to correct this mistake and get rid off the well-established Australian eucalypts. The message out of this would be: do not mix flora or fauna from different areas.

The leaves of the eucalypt are nutritious to only one animal, the koala, which cultivates its own stomach-bacteria to be able to digest the leaves only from special eucalypt trees. Termites and ants have developed their own process of breaking down eucalypt leaf material in Australia. Ants compost eucalypt leaves in an anthill, leaving the job to bacteria to undo nutrients for their digestion, an important symbiosis of nature to control its waste.

An interesting aspect of the eucalypt tree is also that water taken out of the ground is partly evaporated into the air, especially at night, which creates the so-important cycle for rain. One tarpaulin over the top of a tree and one on the ground can deliver water overnight. Collected on the ground tarpaulin it can help somebody to survive in the drought stricken heat of Central Australia. Australian trees are vital for the continent's survival.

Travelling north on the Stuart Highway, not much traffic was met, but drivers often made use of the unlimited speed in the Northern Territory outside populated areas. A road train going 140 km per hour creates an airwave to an oncoming vehicle that needs to be handled with great care.

On one occasion, we pulled over to let a road train pass us. It was going at a very high speed with its three trailers behind. Before it gained any distance from us, a van on the opposite lane got picked up from the wind pressure of the truck and thrown into the air like a feather, ending up on its roof in a ditch on the side of the road.

This was the sudden end of a dream journey for an elderly couple. The road train kept moving, its driver most likely not even realising this incident had occurred. The couple managed to get out of the car wreckage on their own with only a couple of minor cuts and bruises. Everything in the car was a mess. Nobody could smell leaked petrol though, which was a good sign. The next fortuitous thing was the chance arrival of a police patrol car, looking into the incident, so that we didn't have to stay there and were free to continue our trip. The message however was clear; watch out for road trains. In particular, caravans behind a car often become unstable when they pass a big speeding road train.

DUNMARRA

Well before nightfall, Dunmarra became our destination for the day. The usual petrol station with caravan park behind had ample space left for us to stay overnight. This included a much-appreciated shower. We had drawn closer to the Top End of the Northern Territory, which meant we had arrived in the tropics. Temperatures had risen considerably here, remaining on 30 degrees well into the night. The weather was not an issue from now on: only blue skies and warm sunshine in a dry winter air. All the gear needed for the previous cold nights was stored away.

A public telephone across the road surprised us. When calling home to Caboolture the box didn't accept any coins because a previous coin had stuck in the slot, thus keeping the line permanently open. No wonder we were not alone in front of the telephone box. The locals must have known that here were free telephone calls. The free telephone worked for us also, bringing us the good news that the property at home had not burnt down yet! Son Micki was as good as his word and was keeping the place 'alive'

MATARANKA

Arja at Mataranka, Elsey National Park – Northern Territory

Our next destination was Mataranka in Elsey National Park. This national park has its own history going back to 1912, when Mrs. Aeneas Gunn lived with her husband on this former cattle station, describing her life with the Aborigines in her book 'We of the Never Never'. Mrs. Gunn escaped from the civilized life of the city into this outback station, experiencing at first hand the demands of life there. Today it is changed. Civilisation has also reached Elsey National Park, the name alone keeping its heritage alive.

Arriving at the park, it was hard to believe that this was wintertime, as the temperature remained well above 30 degrees Celsius into the night. Here, Mataranka introduced us to a tropical oasis. Only a few kilometres off the Stuart Highway to the east, a cabbage palm forest surrounded a developed thermal pool, leaving the dry land from further south behind. A complete service centre at some distance from the thermal oasis offered shopping facilities, a motel, a caravan park and even entertainment. The place had become a magnet for tourists.

Under eucalypt trees on the caravan site, plenty of space was left for us to find a site that suited us. A log barrier limited the area outside, where dry grass was cut short to avoid accidental fires. Further out, the Top End wilderness again took hold. Next to the cabbage palm oasis in the north past the Roper River, several signs reminded us to stay away from the river because in the Top End, crocodiles were hiding in any place where there was water.

The sun hadn't set behind the horizon yet, allowing us to make our first visit to the artesian pool, which was located in the middle of the cabbage palm forest. The footpath to the pool lay slightly higher above the forest's floor, which was covered with dry, fallen palm leaves away from the path. All around, pointed fan-shaped leaves nearly closed out the sky above, retreating once the pool area was reached. The palm sanctuary is so far unique; it holds the original gene pool of all cabbage palms, another significant biological oasis of Australia.

The embankment of the pool was set in stone, making a stable path for people going in and out of it. We were not alone; many travellers had come the short walking distance from the park to this natural health Mecca. The water equalled the outside temperature of 35 degrees. Besides the rich mineral composition of the water, a sulphuric smell filled the air. Through a hidden pocket of the oval-shaped pool came new thermal spring water constantly bubbling in from an underground point. It is said that the origin of this water is as far away as the Queensland

Tablelands, from where it disappears underground, travelling all the way between a massive sandstone-plateau of the north, and finally emerging here from underground as a constant thermal fountain.

Martin at the Mataranka thermal pool

At the fountain, the temperature was still higher than the 35 degrees of the pool, cooling down gradually on its passage into the main basin. Swimming for a limited time in this mineral water activates blood circulation and organ functions, as long as this is not overdone. Everybody has to know what is good for him and not turn a stimulating effect into a debilitating one.

The pool with its mineral water was safe from crocodile predators. However they lay patiently under water for the incautious tourist in the nearby Roper River. Keeping away from crocodile infested waters is a must, because they are unpredictable and have survived far longer than man has.

Buses arrived late into the night giving passengers either a short stopover on their tour to the south or accommodating them for the night. Back in the park, known musicians entertained the park's visitors well into the night, performing Australian country music. Nobody could sleep as long as the music went on. Therefore it was best to join in, take a seat around the many tables and enjoy this modern addition to the outback with an Aussie beer and dinner from the restaurant behind.

Returning to our spot in the park, we found kangaroos had come from the adjacent bush forests, watching curiously to see what was going on. They only came a certain distance, then retreated quickly into the darkness of the night. Flying foxes cut through the air skillfully between the high-standing eucalypt trees of the park. The night's temperature dropped slightly just before dawn, inviting flocks of birds to the scene. They waited up in the trees, but came down to us as soon as we had started our breakfast.

Bush birds visiting Mataranka

Grey-brown, black-spotted birds in their hundreds came down to the ground in front of us. While the majority of them quarrelled for seemingly nothing, individual birds advanced and gained more and more confidence until one of them made the push on to our hands, stealing its reward. However, when returning to the flock on the ground, it faced a battle for its takings. The message travelled fast, until we found ourselves surrounded by birds, which tried to catch even the wheat biscuits we spooned into our mouths. Clever individual birds escaped with their takings high up into the trees, returning only for another go. The only way to gain our freedom was to store all food away. Having done this, the birds returned into the trees watching out for their next 'victim'.

Little lorikeet parrots with their colourful plumage, exhibiting almost every known colour, started their day on a leaking water tap, not far from our location. While a lorikeet flock mucked around on the top lever, only one at a time went underneath it collecting the released drops from the leaking tap. They also made sure that nothing was wasted.

Lorikeet parrots, Mataranka

Colourful beauty

This feeding frenzy attracted other birds: one kookaburra and a raven, which caused confusion and some panic in the birds' world, making all the others disappear into the high eucalypt canopies. During the night, kangaroos returned to the park, remaining in hiding for most of the day when the temperature soared.

After one full rest day in Elsey National Park our tour continued the next morning. The short distance back to the Stuart Highway was covered quickly. Straight after the park, dry land took over. Farm properties appeared on the way, where a milk can hung horizontal between two timber logs, making up the traditional outback letterbox. Also, the name of the homestead is usually engraved on a timber plank, fixed on a timber log above ground. No house could be seen; only a dusty track pointed in the direction of a homestead. Some of them were quite a distance out in the country and consisted mainly of huge cattle stations.

Road flood sign

A bridge crossing a deep creek bed had a water level sign on the side of the road, starting with a zero in the creek and marking up to 6 metres in height. This meant that any water level at the descent point indicated what the level down at the creek was after a good summer storm, making you think twice about whether to keep going or not.

KATHERINE

Katherine, the third largest city of the Northern Territory, was not too far in the distance to the north along the Stuart Highway. From the Kimberley region in the west a major arterial road, the Victoria Highway, joins the Stuart Highway at Katherine, which makes it an important economic centre.

A main road leads through the town with its centre parking like most country towns. Besides the usual banks and shopping facilities, stores with special stockman's gear could be found here and there. Farmers, stockmen, and farm labourers from far away properties don't arrive here too often. They come to stock up on boots, stockman's hats with wide brims, shirts, trousers and tools. During their stay in town they try to make the trip worthwhile by catching up with people too. The town becomes a meeting point for country men and women. Many bring along their stories in exchange for news on the footpath, inside a shop and most certainly in the town's pubs. Aborigines are also around in numbers on footpaths, in shops and everywhere else. They are either locals or come from outside, mixing into the life of a pulsing country town.

The summer before, the whole town and its surroundings were submerged in the floodwaters of the Katherine River. What was hard to comprehend, when looking at the riverbed on the northern outskirts, was how deep the water had been running here between the massive rock boulders.

Besides shopping for groceries in town, we bought for each of us a real Australian 'Cobb & Co' leather stockman's hat as used out in the bush. A stockman's hat is an effective way to keep the strong sun off the head. Fitted out with everything we needed, our tour continued outside Katherine to the east through dry country again. Farm properties of smaller sizes lined the road looking rather deplorable in the midst of the dry season. Looking at some of them, it could be suggested that property developers would be quick to find a buyer when the owner was no longer able to maintain it.

Not everybody stands up to the demands of working a country property. A lot of continued hard work has to go into it first, before any owner's pride could come out of it. Where water for irrigation was not used, there was no green to be seen; only Australian bush and eucalypt trees defied drought conditions. A billabong near the road harboured on its shallow banks a Jabiru, the Territory's national emblem, screening the mud for food with its long bill. The Jabiru belongs to the stork family, its plumage is more glossy green-black than its mainly white European counterpart. It takes the hotter weather conditions in its stride.

Jabiru - Northern Territory

NITMILUK NATIONAL PARK - KATHERINE GORGE

Katherine Gorge

On our current route from Katherine we were not far from Nitmiluk National Park - 5221 kilometres from our hometown in southeast Queensland. Nitmiluk is one of the many outback oases in the continent. Each oasis is unique and Nitmiluk is extra special. It is the 'Grand Canyon' of Australia with one major difference - Nitmiluk lies in the tropics and its gorges are filled with the Katherine River water, leaving rocky banks to rise vertically above it.

The road took us to a visitors' centre before descending to the start of the gorges.

Despite winter being in full swing, the temperature during the day was 41 degrees Celsius in the shade, as shown on the visitors' board.

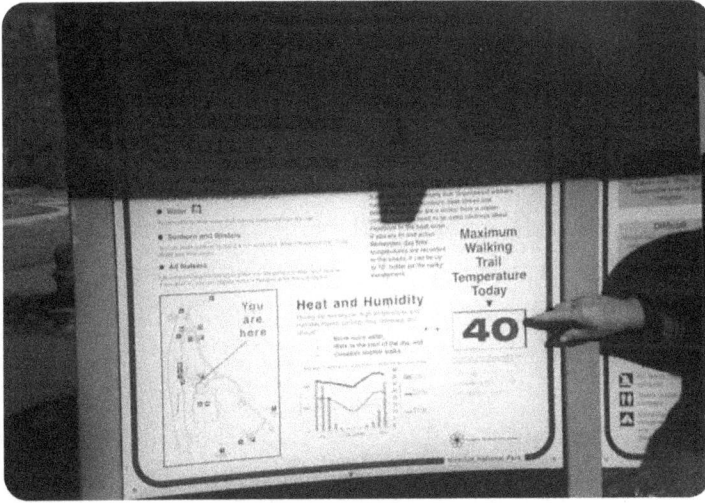

Visitors' centre sign - 40 degrees Celsius

The sky was completely free of clouds. The visitors' centre offered a stay to recover from the outside heat, which rose even higher in the rock crevices of the canyon. Most people waited here for a boat to tour the canyons in comfort. A well-organized parking area was located in front of the centre to accommodate large numbers of vehicles.

Indigenous art worker

At the entrance under flourishing bush, a number of Aborigines sat in the shade working on their paintings and giving visitors an insight into how they create their beautiful art works. The work was quite original, but prices were inflated for tourists' budgets. Our plan was to spend one day exploring the top of the canyons on foot, and then another day exploring the water the whole length of the canyon with a proper tourist boat. Nobody could afford to forget that this was crocodile territory and there was no room for any mistakes like taking a swim or exploring on foot along the canyon's banks.

On the day after our arrival, a small stony footpath took us not far from the visitors' centre up into the rock cliffs. Equipped with our 'Cobb & Co' sun hat, firm shoes, good sunscreen, a backpack carrying bread, biscuits, oranges and most of all drinking water in a thermos flask, we set out. A first aid kit was also not forgotten, because on the visitors' board it was stated, 'Excursions on foot into the rock cliffs of the canyons require fitness in extreme temperature conditions. Snakes are likely to be encountered.' Keeping this in mind could only help us to prepare better for this first part of our Nitmiluk adventure.

On the steep way up through crevices, bush established a firm hold in the rocks along the canyon's side. Views of the water broke through more and more often the higher the path went. Near the top we had to go inland first across a deeply carved rock plateau, where in the crevices active bush and tree life had firmly taken a hold, creating here and there flourishing oases despite the winter drought.

Arja at the rock plateau - Nitmiluk

Martin at the rock plateau - Nitmiluk

On the first peak of the cliffs a huge round tank had been built containing treated water for the visitors' centre down at the entrance to the gorges. Water was pumped through a pipe system up into the tank as required, running from there in separate pipes down to the centre without the need of constant power. The properly fenced plant kept everybody out of it.

A walk on the rock plateau led in places to the edge of the canyon, delivering views across to the other side, where scattered eucalypt forest continued into the interior.

No vegetation could take a foothold on the vertical rock faces, only in crevices and in some places along the riverbanks. The water in the canyon lay calm and dark, deep down. Taking the time to watch this soon revealed that under that calm surface, crocodiles waited patiently. On the leeside of a river bend a strip of sandy beach emerged at the bottom of rock walls. It was here that crocodiles lay in the sun soaking up the heat. They were unmistakably visible and remained outside the water, until one of the canyon cruise boats arrived when they disappeared as quickly as lightning into their river hideout.

Believe it or not, we saw from the cliffs some people taking a plunge from the opposite riverbank, despite crocs rushing back into the water. A distance would be no issue for crocs to overcome; this was playing with one's own life; there would be no escape from a croc attack. We were alone on the rock cliffs and enjoyed the views each time we gained access from inland. In shallow depressions, vivid plant life of native bush, low trees and grass indicated water build up during heavy summer storms.

The temperature in such places waited to 'cook' everything that came into it. When it was 41 degrees around the visitors' centre, it was not far from 50 degrees here, reminding us to move out very quickly to the cliff edge above the canyon, where a slight breeze kept the air constantly circulating. Despite the heat, changing views from the high above position became an experience that was still superior to an aerial view out of a helicopter, because during our walk everything happened at a relatively slow pace, giving us enough time to absorb the constantly changing scenery.

Helicopter flights were also available, a quicker way to gain views of Nitmiluk. On foot however between the few plant-islands on the rock plateau, palms like the red lantana, a true Top End specimen, could be found, while mainly banksias made up the majority of other plants. The absence of proper soil allowed a red lantana to grow only very thin reddish branches and fan-shaped, sharp pointed reddish-green leaves.

The region here is called, the 'door to the Kimberley', which stretches to the west, building up an original, ancient, natural environment of its own. Not only the land has a long history, but also its flora, especially the boab trees, which can be found in Nitmiluk. Very few hamlets and farms were established on the fringe of its land, making it one of the most isolated places on earth, also one of the hottest.

Returning in 1983 from Perth in Western Australia to Brisbane in Queensland through the north of Australia, we crossed the Kimberley Region and experienced a transformation into another hardly explored world. The only road had been washed completely away by ferocious storms, which sometimes happens after years of a dry spell, while the moisture stays consistently in the air making the humid life here a real challenge.

KIMBERLEY REGION

The Kimberley Region is mainly located in the north of Western Australia but extends into the Top End of the Northern Territory. Its grasslands change in its heartland into some of the earth's oldest land formations: plateaus, bush, ancient colourful weather-beaten rounded mountainous elevations, isolated or in chains.

Flora like the boab trees reminds us of a connection with Madagascar and Ecuador before the continents shifted. The boab trees of Ecuador embodied in ancient Inca mythology the meaning of eternal life. A particular boab tree can be found in the Kimberley, on the trunk of which is engraved a year, the number dating back almost 200 years, and which can still be seen today because of the slow growth of the tree. Nobody really knows what age boab trees can reach.

Only a few pioneers shared with a few Aborigines a hidden beauty found only in the Australian Kimberley. Today's bus tours to Broome on the Indian Ocean can give only a quick impression of what is concealed in its centre from the fringe of its land.

A tour in the Kimberleys still requires four-wheel drive experience and an independent enterprising spirit. There isn't much room for error when exploring the Kimberleys. From our position up on the cliffs of Nitmiluk looking west, we could see the Kimberleys located in the far distance, memories of an unparalleled natural wilderness.

Returning to the visitors' centre we had to come down a ravine, where trees had grown twisted from raging storm waters during summer. Finally down from the plateau of the rock walls and with the baking heat left behind, we realised how tired we had become during the day's excursion. We suddenly realised that we had taken no pictures of both of us together, because nobody else had been up there. With night progressing, some relief arrived through the cooler air. Kangaroos came from the darkness of the bush, so close that we could pat them. We found out how soft their dense short fur was. The head of a kangaroo is definitely like that of a roe, but this is where the similarity ends.

For the next day we had planned to visit Nitmiluk by boat and look at the scenery from the canyon's waters. The first early boat took us on board after a longish waiting period ashore under the acacia trees. Here bats had gathered in their thousands, hanging inside the trees on branches with their heads down and their wings wrapping around their whole body. Their constant sharp cries meant it was difficult to hear even one single word on the ground. "This is our territory." Was this their message?

Sunshine slowly increased the heat, while all these black creatures with their brown fox-like little heads, the body hidden between the wings, have settled in the acacia trees for a rest during the day, returning later to make their incredible noise after dusk. The boat easily made her passage through the canyon, being driven steadily by a pounding diesel engine. Rocky bounds changed constantly into rapid rises; the water laid calm, and silvery ripples shone where the sun entered the canyon.

During the boat tour, crocodiles had disappeared into the canyon's deep waters long before the boat's arrival. Nobody made any attempt to lean across the railing to look more closely at crocodiles. The tour was split into two parts because now, during winter, the water level dropped in the canyon and didn't allow the boat to pass a rock barrier. Everyone had to disembark and walk the distance across, where a second boat waited on the other side to continue the tour in the canyon.

The boat stopped in front of a niche in a rock wall. After everything had turned completely silent, the boat's captain called the name of a turtle and not long after, it popped up on the surface swimming freely around the boat as long as everything remained silent. The voice of another person made the turtle disappear instantly into the underwater cave. An echo from the niche amplified the slightest sound.

Views from the opposite direction created new impressions of the canyon. Our vision became limited sometimes because of the rising rock walls sending across their coloured reflections, which varied between dark shades and bright sunny spots. When getting closer, another sudden view opened into a new passage. The round trip took nearly four hours and we were able to experience the magnificent views of Nitmiluk from the comfort of the boat. The boat tour rounded off impressions for us from more than one perspective and left us with lasting memories. The road that had brought us all those thousands of kilometres from Brisbane to Nitmiluk displayed a destination that still remains special. There won't be any other Nitmiluk.

Returning to the Stuart Highway, our journey continued further north towards Darwin, the capital of the Northern Territory. Eucalypt forests on both sides of the road became denser. Fires had left widespread trails mainly on the ground vegetation. In some places everything was turned into black ashes. Eucalypt trees can survive fires only when subjected not too long to the heat. Loose bark on the trunks assists the fire to move away from the tree. Also, here nature was largely primed for fires, demonstrating how regeneration can transform a fire-stricken area into fresh life.

Some of the first new shoots were sago palms and cardboard plants. Their brilliant light green new leaves stuck out of the black surroundings.

Roadside - Northern Territory

Termite country, Top End – Northern Territory

Many termite mounds also regularly survive fires, emerging each time stronger, when newly 'baked'. The further north we came, the taller the termite mounds grew with the increasing heat. The land gave impressions of being on another planet. No wonder Charles Darwin became inspired 150 years earlier about the region that inspired his evolution theory, in which every living form is subjected to cycles determining through adaptation a survival of species. Darwin also created through his vision the premise: 'Survival of only the fittest', which is a realistic formula for life in Australia. The capital of the Northern Territory has adopted Darwin's name in recognition of the outstanding contribution he delivered to a fundamental understanding of nature.

EMERALD SPRINGS

One of the towns we passed through on the road to Darwin was Emerald Springs, a tiny hamlet between rocky hillsides. A huge mango tree invited us to rest under its shady canopy. Pigs in a nearby enclosure must have noted our arrival and started in their unique 'pig language' to tell us their stories, but we really couldn't translate. However the owner appeared on the scene, "You must like my mango tree; is there anything you need?"

"We are fine and enjoying the cool shade under your tree. Do you have any objections to us resting here?"

"Don't you worry; you're fine. It just doesn't happen very often that somebody stops in our small place; everybody on the road is in a hurry today. You must have come a long way to our Top End. Now is the right time to see it, because the weather is neither too hot nor too humid. In summer, life sometimes turns difficult here, but when winter arrives, everything is quickly forgotten. Now our biggest concern is ensuring that nobody starts a fire in the dry season. On the property I keep the grass green with daily irrigation, but beyond that, the grass is like a tinderbox. A cigarette from a passing car or the glass debris of a beer bottle that refracts sunlight, can easily lead to an inferno. Please don't do this to us."

"Your place is so well looked after; we promise not to do anything wrong by you."

"I'll leave you to it. I have to go and do something; my work is not going away. Have a safe trip."

"Thanks for your kindness and stay well."

"That's good thinking; I'll try my 'worst'."

Termite mounds became more frequent and grew higher the more we advanced northwards; temperature and moisture in the air had also risen. The different colours of the mounds seen at a distance already gave an indication of the soil composition, varying from dark red and light brown to grey. Closer to Darwin in Litchfield Park and Kakadu, colonies of special termite mounds can be looked at, which give interesting information on their creation and their 'builders'. Ants, including their termite relatives, can be considered the best-organized living form on earth.

Our aim now was to reach Darwin on the same day. An above ground pipe system followed on both sides of the road, carting water to Darwin. Darwin is said to have the best water quality of all cities in Australia. The reason is the intense summer storm season of the Top End. Then the excess water seeps into the ground, is filtered and stored in the huge sandstone layers of the region. Water taken from there is as pure as only these natural conditions can deliver. In the future, it will have to be closely monitored so that no contamination of this treasured source occurs. Once contaminated, it won't ever be the same for the rest of time.

Closer to Darwin the traffic travelled on a double lane highway. In the flat country of the coastal area appeared the Territory's mango farms. Mango trees were planted here like big, dark-green 'mushroom heads' in exact coordinated rows, bearing fruit much earlier than further south, from where we had come. The yellow, red, and green colours of the fruits' outer skin shone plentifully through the dense canopy; it must have been the Kensington Pride variety, sold mainly overseas from here.

Picking this first class mango crop is a constant problem because of the small population in the Territory. Besides that, mango picking in September/October is not an easy job; mangoes have sticky sap on the skin, which can irritate sensitive human skin. This is exacerbated by the legendary heat build-up during springtime. Mangoes are one of the most valuable fruits containing a high percentage of vitamin C. Mangoes from the Top End are classified as top of the range, selling well every season, as long as they are picked and sent quickly to the overseas markets.

Students of the Northern Territory University often help out with the harvesting, earning themselves a few extra 'bob'. The extremes of the weather in the Top End are harsh: six months bone-dry during winter and the other six months of the build-up and wet season during the summer. This sticky, muggy hot weather during the so-called build-up is called 'mango-madness': mangoes love it, while the heat can easily drive people mad. Later on during our journey we also visited a model mango farm in North Queensland, where we learnt how difficult it is to preserve the mango freshness.

DARWIN

Welcome to Darwin – Northern Territory

A large sign on the outskirts of Darwin welcomed the traveller. The city has been rebuilt since cyclone Tracey destroyed it in 1974. Today, an exhibition near the coast shows the events as they happened: underpinned by a cyclone sound-fury in pictures as close as possible to the real thing, recreating parts of the scenery. Today's newly rebuilt Darwin has a simple layout: the airport is located in its centre, a main road leads around it with connecting side-streets to all suburbs and a main arterial along the coast links through the side-streets back again to the city.

At the time of Cyclone Tracey, Darwin's population was 80 000 - in city terms not a big place. Interestingly, the Northern Territory doesn't count its population per square kilometre, but the other way round, so many square kilometres per person. In 2001 each 'Territorian' could claim 8.5 square kilometres. It should also be mentioned that at that time, the Territory held twenty times more cattle than people. When looking at the natural resources, it has to be one of the richest places on earth. Living in the Top End of the Northern Territory remains a challenge to this day, mostly because of its climatic conditions.

Many houses in Darwin today have climate control, which cannot be supplied in many workplaces, making work especially difficult to handle on building sites. To attract a work force, wages are generally higher than elsewhere. With the summer's arrival, the legendary 'build up' in humidity, heat and still air causes a partial exodus of the population every year to the southeastern states of the continent. Before winter, many return to the dry sunny conditions of the Top End. There is unofficial recognition that if you have lived 5 consecutive years in Darwin, you have proved you are 'tough'. People that can stand up to such demands find good opportunities in the Northern Territory. A small population, vast territory and natural wealth beg for more people to share this unique life.

Our youngest daughter Gucki had chosen to study at the Darwin University, also a unique place. Its campus consists of a modern satellite building-layout with large tropical landscaped areas in between. Students enjoyed the open spaces and as their numbers were relatively small in relation to the facilities, a rare study climate could be found here. The quality of teaching was guaranteed through international representation balancing university requirements with the qualified local staff.

Our daughter rented a cheap unit, which was very difficult to do in Darwin. Prices were generally high, because most goods arrived from outside the Territory. There are not enough people to financially support the maintenance of quality infrastructure. The unit easily accommodated us as well as Gucki thus solving our accommodation problems. In the back of the ground floor unit a bamboo fence bordered a small yard, where a table surrounded by chairs invited us during the cooler hours of the evening.

Our car was converted from a touring vehicle into a car more suitable for the city traffic. A trip to the city along the coast showed many beautiful tropical gardens around houses. Water seemed to be in abundance, as everything was kept green even throughout the dry winter season; frangipani shone in white, pink, red and mixed colours through the dark-green long leaves, and palms often rose higher than houses, giving a much needed shade with their bushy leaf crowns.

Along the shore promenade between short green lawns on both sides of the footpaths, stood hardy Bismarck palms. Pedestrians, bicycle riders, joggers and picnickers found ample spaces here on the seaside. The Timor Sea lay calm, no waves visible, but signs warned of the deadly jellyfish and saltwater crocodiles. Nobody could be seen in the water, only in a pool near the beach. Mansions on the city side of the beach road had fabulous views into the gardens along the beach and to the shiny Timor Sea.

Bismarck palm promenade - Darwin

A short, steep slope separated the partly sandy and stony stretch of beach from the green grounds. Close to the city, Government House could be seen on a beach elevation in midst of a marvellous tropical garden. The old building is said to be one of the only surviving buildings of cyclone Tracey in 1974; it must have been exceptional workmanship. The Parliament Building and Supreme Court opposite Government House were each on a separate massive high building block, where tall column facades were raised outside to protect them from cyclonic weather.

Parliament - Darwin

Not far away were the Botanical Gardens located on a slight hillside. Mainly huge, old trees spread their shade over most of the area turning it into a park for relaxing walks. Glasshouses in the same terrain showed specialized cultured flora from forests and bush out of the Top End. One more place of interest was the Arts Museum, where - besides fauna and flora - a well-organized exhibition of contemporary Aboriginal artwork could be found – well worth a visit.

On the weekend, near the city centre, there was a market set up over a number of streets and offering lots of homemade goods at bargain prices. The crowd reflected the multicultural makeup of Darwin. Men and women, young and old, Indonesian, South-East Asian and Chinese descent used their bargaining skills in their colourful booths. One could easily imagine being removed to an environment somewhere in Asia. Aborigines were however less likely to be met in the city; they preferred to live closer to their traditional Land Trusts.

The city centre itself was a layout of modern buildings rising to a limited height because of the cyclonic conditions during summer. Chessboard-like roads led in and out of the centre. Besides the usual banks, shopping centres, speciality shops, hotels, an inner city pedestrian-zone and tropical landscaping along green grass areas, there were also tall palms competing with the high buildings and giving Darwin its special tropical look. All city traffic was directed around the airfield area. After the first day familiarizing ourselves with Darwin, we were able to locate Gucki's address in Rapid Creek northeast of the city centre, quickly and easily from the circular arterial main road. A huge mahogany tree in the corner of the street indicated unmistakably where to turn off to the unit.

The temperature during the day remained consistently at 35 degrees, dropping during the night to barely under 30 degrees, making most of the night rather uncomfortable to sleep. People therefore stayed up longer into the night. The beach promenade with its long wide green lawn could be reached from our location on foot and was a popular destination for many.

Sunset over the Timor Sea - Darwin

Here the sunset created a unique spectacle. In the haze above the horizon, the sun set in a red-yellow disc turning more and more to a magnified darker red ball, sending the last daylight colours in little ripples across the Timor Sea. This turned the sea darker closely followed by the darkening of the sky. Under the Bismarck palms many 'Territorians' had arrived for the day's end. Some had brought chairs and tables from home, fitting them with white tablecloths, arranging fine chinaware and champagne glasses elegantly on the tables and sitting down in their fine 'glad rags'. A repast was enjoyed and in one case a CD player played Bach's 'Brandenburg Concertos' in this tropical garden with views to the beach and further into the sea, while the sun sank in a colourful spectacle behind the horizon. People here understood how to celebrate with nature and that's all that eventually could be said - a typical Darwin atmosphere!

Our daughter Gucki introduced us on another day to the university. We were given the opportunity to participate in a number of lectures during the course of the day. Memories of our student time resurfaced.

When making comparisons, we recalled that in Germany, classes of students were often in their hundreds, whereas here, lectures were attended by twenty to thirty students. In Germany we sometimes had problems seeing and hearing properly because of the distance from the lecturer in the lecture theatre. Here the lecturer addressed a small family of students, so that they could easily communicate. Campus facilities in Darwin were laid out in different matching colours bringing a touch of nature into the buildings. Building complexes were well apart and spaces between were filled with tropical gardens and green meadows. Space seemed to be no problem.

On our first Saturday afternoon in Darwin, Gucki performed her guitar concert – Bach Prelude 999, Villa-Lobos Prelude Nr.1, Study in E-Minor, Prelude Nr. 3 - in the concert hall of the University Campus. It was her first public concert; her performance was outstanding. She played professionally, dressed in a Spanish dress and without music sheets. This was one item on our to-do list, which had triggered the decision to go on the road to Nitmiluk and Kakadu. Having seen Gucki play, we could now cross this off the list. From now on we were free to explore more of the Top End, away from Darwin.

HOWARD SPRINGS

We started with the nearest places of interest so that we could return to Darwin towards the evening and catch up with our daughter, who had to attend her university lectures through the day. Our first destination was Howard Springs, a lake resort in a eucalypt forest in the flat coastal area just outside Darwin. People came here for a picnic and swim, because of its closeness to the city and because there were no crocodiles in the water. Everywhere else in the Top End, signs warned about the danger of crocs.

Barramundi fish swam here, some of which had reached sizes of well over one metre in length. They kept to themselves without endangering anybody despite their size. Not only does the barramundi flesh taste good, but it has also kept up very interesting instincts from an ancient evolution's epoch. The barramundi changes sex from male to female when, during the year's seasons, instinct tells it to swim upriver and change back to male on the return journey downriver. Such mutation happens in freshwater to secure the upbringing of the spawn in an environment of fewer predators. The spawn faces nature's accidental selection for survival on its downstream journey. Barramundi live at times in mixed fresh and seawater. Its migration instinct is similar to that of the salmon, the main difference being its strange sex change. Has nature found here its own formula for the survival of the species by not requiring the duality of the sexes?

BERRY SPRINGS

Berry Springs – Top End, N.T.

Next point of interest in the vicinity of Darwin became Berry Springs and Wildlife Park. In Berry Springs a watercourse cascades down a small drop out of a eucalypt forest into a basin linking it into a lake. Here were clear signs that crocodiles were likely to be in the water. As quite a large number of visitors enjoyed the rushing waters at the cascade, it appeared, there was no danger of crocs in this particular part of the basin.

Arja at Berry Springs

In the lake however, nobody was seen taking any chances. Crocs can be unpredictable in water as well as on land. During 2007 there was news of an incident, which happened in the Atherton Tablelands, far North Queensland, where a saltwater crocodile confronted a stockman when he came off his horse. The man managed to climb a tree in a hurry, but had to survive a whole week up the tree, while the croc took up permanent position under the tree. It was just by luck that somebody turned up to rescue him.

Experts know to meet a croc on land raises alarm bells, because it is sure to be on a desperate food search. Over short distances a croc can strike on land as quick as lightning, making an escape barely possible. They are fierce predators. It has also happened to campers that a croc inspected their tent despite their location well away from water. Good survival techniques are instincts found especially amongst Australia's flora and fauna. Crocodiles in the north of Australia do not pose a constant danger except to those who ignore basic precautions. Australia's crocs are the only ones in the world living in nature's elements of land, freshwater and saltwater. They should never be underestimated; fatal encounters usually happen through neglect.

We also had a good long swim in Berry Springs, standing under the cascade and experiencing the intense massage from the falling water. Before continuing to the Wildlife Park, wooden tables and benches adjacent to the water invited us to picnic on the lawn in front of the eucalypt forest. What grabbed our attention was that there were people from as far away as Germany - with their small children - who were on a two-week holiday. How they were enjoying this nature's oasis was easy for us to pick up because we understood their language. The kids especially enjoyed themselves just like in their home pool, but with the difference that this was not a man-made pool.

THE WILDLIFE PARK

The Wildlife Park was on a dusty track a few kilometres past Berry Springs. A well-organized reception directed visitors to coaches to tour the park. We found it more interesting however to stay on foot and be more independent during our park visit. The whole area, including a large billabong, lay once more in a eucalypt forest.

Dingos at the Wildlife Park – Top End, N.T.

Dingos, Australia's wild dogs, staged their own show with a trainer. The demonstration was quite detailed on their origin and behaviour patterns, which were similar to wolves in a pack. However, if domesticated, they can become the best pet imaginable. The dingo has relatively long legs, a pointed head and light brown fur. DNA research has found that the purest dingo breed roams in the wilderness of the Top End because of having lived a more isolated existence than anywhere else in Australia.

Other places of interest at the park were a huge aviary built into the forest and a terrarium. Aviary visitors entered through a double door and could peacefully watch the Top End's incredibly colourful world of birds. Australia is a bird's paradise. Here birds have survived until recently in large numbers, which is an important natural 'protection mechanism'– birds in a flock confuse a predator more easily than individual birds do. In the outback I have seen birds of prey attack a flock of wild birds but in the midst of the confusion they didn't get even one of them.

In the wide-open spaces of the Australian continent, flocks of galahs, cockatoos, finches and budgerigars can be found. However, in the protection of forests and the few remaining pockets of ancient rainforests along the eastern coastal fringes of the continent, including bush areas and wetlands, more individual bird life can exist - the king parrot, cassowary, jabiru, brush turkey, lorikeets, rosellas, frogmouth, kookaburra, honey eaters, robins, owls, catbird, just to mention a few. Australia certainly has a rich bird life - a bird-lover's paradise.

I remember an incident during the visit of a German family with us. We took them into the rainforest of the Sunshine Coast hinterland, not far from our hometown, Caboolture. While entering the calm of the dense rainforest, our guests followed their usual habit of lighting a cigarette and they had nothing better to say than, "In Germany birds sing more beautifully." How wrong people can be when judging in haste! The season of the year in the Southern hemisphere was of course winter, which gave nature a rest-time before an explosion of new life in the summer to come. To listen to birds in nature, we have to enter their territory virtually unnoticed, only then will their rich sounds be heard. Cigarettes and ringing voices won't encourage birds to sing. The remark that 'in Germany birds sing more beautifully' has since become a saying in our private family vocabulary, which means something is controversial.

A terrarium within the Wildlife Park showed visitors snakes and lizards in humid hot conditions behind glass. Australia is home to most of the venomous snakes in the world; it is always good to leave them alone. They are very effective in defending themselves for whatever reason; that's why they have survived for so long. Some lizards are surprising with their colourful collars showing their sudden transformation to frighten off an enemy. Nature has given these creatures all possible 'tools' to defend themselves in order to survive. In a rapidly changing world, we should still respect such ancient living forms, which are likely to survive longer than us, if we are not intelligent enough and adapt better to nature's course.

LITCHFIELD NATIONAL PARK

To end the day we continued our drive to Litchfield National Park. The short cut back to the Stuart Highway didn't really pay off, because of very bad road conditions. As the track also went through puddles of water, the car received its own mud bath from the red-muddy soil. This was the first time our vehicle changed its appearance in the outback. Dirt from outside could be cleaned off again - the main thing was, we didn't become stuck in the outback mud.

The sun had already started to set on the horizon when we arrived in the parking area near Wangi Falls in Litchfield National Park. A caravan park was in the surrounding eucalypt forest and bush land, which led to rocky cliffs around a lake where there was a waterfall. The trapped heat of the day did not allow the night's cooler air to move in before dawn. The park was filled with visitors; we nearly missed out on a permit to stay with our car. Others had caravans, and some tents were also put up on the ground. Due to the proximity of the Wangi-Falls, caution was needed because, where there is water there are also snakes.

Wangi Falls - Litchfield Park, Top End, N.T.

A constant light mist in the air from the falls had kept the immediate surroundings fresh and green even through the dry winter season. Especially during the night the area became a magnet for wildlife. Kangaroos hopped between people's resting places, as everything turned silent in the place. The few people that remained in the open could occasionally nearly touch a kangaroo, which was mainly after the green grass.

Curiosity and the smell of leftovers from barbecues even brought the dingos cautiously in. They remained however at a safe distance and could only be seen from time to time. Crickets were busy emitting their chirping throughout the night.

Early next morning after a hot sleepless night, we started to explore Wangi Falls before the sun brought back the day's heat.

On the lower section of the rocky hillside a footpath started to go up steeper and steeper on the side to the fall's top edge through a small 'pandanus-spiralis' forest. The 'pandanus-spiralis' owes its name to the spiral growth in the centre and branches with long, thin, flabelliform leaves. Tiny thorns along the leaf edges protect the plant from curious 'visitors', including humans. Thorns in the hand become instantly itchy and are very difficult to remove, because of their small flexible size. The spiral- growth of a pandanus serves to strengthen the stem and direct rainwater from its outer leaf-areas to the plant's roots in the ground.

Further up on the footpath the forest gave way to lower bush, which again almost entirely disappeared on the top rock plateau. In two separate places, water currents from inland pushed their way through crevices towards the edge of the vertical rock wall, approximately 80 metres above the lake's basin. Views from up there stretched to the northwest coast across a vast eucalypt forest. The views were great, but extreme caution was needed to stay safely away from the wet slippery rock faces, especially near the falls' edge.

Even for the most daring, a jump down to the basin would be suicide. Next to the falls on the opposite side of our ascent, a footpath led downwards through increasingly dense bush, changing into a forest. After a hot walk, a swim in the falls' basin could not come quickly enough. The number of people in the area was most likely a deterrent for crocodiles. People in the refreshingly cool water must have found out already whether or not crocs were in the basin. This encouraged us to join them.

Florence Falls - Litchfield, N.T.

Cooled down from a swim, another waterfall in Litchfield, Florence Falls, became our target. In the distance to these falls a small current pushed its way through a rocky bed in the scattered eucalypt forest. A parking area close by attracted most visitors to the water to cool down and have a picnic. The footpath following the watercourse led to a high outlook opposite the two side-by-side main falls. Underneath, the current out of a basin to the north continued into the coastal Top End. The scenery was breathtaking: fresh tinges of green forest leaves, yellow-brown-reddish rock, water rushing out of the forest to the edge and falling in curtains down into a basin open only to the north.

The basin must have been deep enough to allow two daredevils to jump from a rock column all the way down into the basin. Despite its lower height compared with Wangi Falls, the 40 metres still required courage and skills for a successful jump. Views from a narrow platform, which was secured by a steel bar fence told of its depth in the deep, rocky gorge of dark, calm waters. Further inland, outside the gorge, treetops of eucalypt forest formed a light green carpet against an azure sky.

On this excursion, the day passed more quickly than anticipated, introducing swarms of mosquitos at dusk. For a change our rest place for the night ended up away from the road in the neighbourhood of bush, next to a brook. The night remained completely silent. Before dawn, kangaroos came very close out of curiosity, showing no haste, no fear and with first daylight the birds' singing filled the forest canopy echoing constantly through the air. Nature's wake-up call signalled a new day for us.

Wildlife visitor at night

Termite Mound - Litchfield, N.T. with family members

On our return to the highway leading to Darwin, a tree farm of tropical timbers was halfway established - a great idea begging duplication. The investment to plant a mahogany tree is said to return a higher profit than traditional investments can deliver over many years. This could become the saviour of nature's virgin forests if we were prepared to wait for a first harvest. However the stumbling block is that we rarely give ourselves time to succeed long term in anything we do.

The tree farm was established in rows numbered for each tree specimen. A variation in height and new plantations pointed towards a systematic increase in tree numbers during recent years. A good fence deterred closer inspection; therefore it was impossible to identify the different rows, especially because they were all very young and not yet showing their more mature characteristics. The only clear identification that could be seen from close-by rows was a sign with the name of the mahogany tree.

Flora in tropical climates has to be more resilient in many more ways than in temperate climates. It needs to handle termites, heat, cold, wet, dry and consequently a unique hardwood is often the result.

The great grandchildren of today's tree farmers will have the benefit of a rich harvest and when the replanting is continued, a steady return on this investment could ensure the future of the natural environment. I will not see the mahogany trees ready for harvesting in my lifetime, but one or two generations further on will have with each mature tree a capital of approximately fifty thousand dollars in today's currency; likely to be much more by then.

KAKADU

To get to the road towards our next destination, Kakadu, we had to go back in the direction of Darwin. Before reaching Darwin however, the Arnhem Highway turned off to the east at Humpty Doo. Then the road led straight into Kakadu National Park. Not long after, there was a bridge spanning the Adelaide River in the midst of the flat country of the Wetlands. Surprisingly, the river carried a lot of water despite the dry winter season. On a hillside in these flat Wetlands a tourist centre, called 'Window on the Wetlands', informed us about the diverse fauna and flora of this particular area.

World Heritage Kakadu National Park

In geological terms the flood plains of Kakadu are very young. Cahill's Plain in front of the Ubirr lookout is only 800 years old. The plains have always provided a welcome array of foods for the indigenous population - fruit, seeds, roots, stems of lilies, yams, yegge and gurrung.

Flocks of magpie geese, spoonbills, brolgas, glossy ibis and the occasional single jabiru could be seen here. The Wetlands are also the main habitat for many frog species. During the early wet, the mating calls of these creatures can be deafening. Where there are frogs it is a sign that the environment is still in order. Annual flooding allows fish to breed in astonishing numbers and disperse throughout the Wetlands in a boom and bust cycle. Fifty-two species of fish have been identified in the

Wetlands, ranging from the tiny freshwater 'blue eyes' to 8 kg salmon-tailed catfish.

Pig-nosed turtle and of course both the freshwater and saltwater crocodiles call the area their home. The freshwater crocodiles are generally found more in the upper reaches of a river, whereas saltwater crocodiles are common in all watercourses from the sea right through to the larger pools in the sandstone gorge country. When young, they eat frogs and small fish, but once they exceed 3 metres in length they begin to take mammals such as wallabies and dingos. Very large crocodiles frequently feed on mammals. The two crocodile species often mix, but the freshwater species must keep a very low profile to survive.

During the wet season from November to May these floodplains explode in a riot of growth: lotus lilies, yellow snowflake flower lilies, mangrove flowers, paperbark, flowers and orchids in pockets of wetland jungles. Back on the road, which could be accessed mainly during the dry season, when water levels have receded, a warning sign strikes the eye: 'Crocs on the road'! Particularly at night they come on the bitumen road surface to soak up the heat generated during the day. It wouldn't be a good move to hit a croc with a car, because the croc would be tougher than the car and could potentially cause a lot of trouble. This is most likely the only place in the world, where such signs are seen on the roadside.

Mary River - Kakadu, N.T.

The next river crossing was at the Mary River, another big river course. The embankment on both sides of the river rose not only high out of the water, but also from the surrounding flat land. Crocodiles could be seen from the road as they rested on the embankment, soaking the sun's heat in. Stopping on the roadside just after the bridge we watched a boat filled with a number of passengers in the middle of the river on a croc-watch tour. As soon as the boat came near the 'sun-baking beach' of the crocs, they rushed in a split second into the river, submerging in its murky waters. They only disappeared though until the boat had gained some distance away. People in the boat attempted to feed the crocs so that they appeared with their nostrils just out of the water. Nothing else could be seen in the greenish murky water and nobody would even try to put a hand into the water, as the crocs would have been instantly on the scene.

It was also not advisable to go on foot near the riverbank. When striking, a crocodile is extremely fast in its watching distance, making escape impossible. Nobody wants to see how a croc grabs and rolls its prey, firmly gripping with its jaws and taking it into pieces in the water. This would be one of the most frightening experiences. A croc's transition from a calm resting position into an aggressive stance, whether it is in the water or on land, is so explosive that it is a must to stay a safe distance away from them.

Fields of pandanus-spiralis with a part of their brownish dry leaf-crowns could be seen along the roadsides giving a wild impression; only the newer growth rose greenly upwards. In some parts fire had raged, leaving everything except the pandanus-trunks in black ashes waiting for the next wet season to shoot new leaf-crowns. There were no houses in the park area on the road to its only settlement, Jabiru, in the far east. A service centre on the road near the Mary River and Kakadu Holiday Village were the only signs of civilisation in the area, which is World Heritage listed.

Another large river - the South Alligator River - turned up further east. Dense mangroves grew along its banks, giving the river a distinct green vegetation line on both sides. We followed a beaten track from the road to the river. Closer to it, a stone set crossing seemed to be a passage to the other riverside. To have a closer look, a solid tree branch hanging over the river's bank invited a climb, but not for long. As soon as I arrived above the water, a croc appeared out of the murky water looking at me.

One of the many Crocodiles in South Alligator River - Kakadu, N.T.

Quicker than the croc would ever have thought, I was back on the riverbank and left the place for our parked car near the road. There is a rule: you should never return to the same spot on a river or a lagoon, because the crocs make their investigations most of the time during a first encounter and are waiting for the next encounter to strike.

JABIRU

Jabiru at the end of the Arnhem Highway is a newly established settlement. In its centre lay a tourist facility of which one particular building was outstanding with a crocodile-shaped roof, indicating from the air that this is croc country. Indigenous Aborigines live here in housing provided by the Northern Territory Government. Jabiru is the starting point to the nearby Ranger Uranium Mine, the richest mine of its kind in the world. It sparked a lot of controversy with its position so close to the World Heritage listed Kakadu National Park.

Money unfortunately drives this part of the world. Mining activities on a huge open cut scale have changed the area with its installations of dumps and artificial storage dams. Expansion is a heated ongoing debate, because radioactive materials have already leaked into the environment. 'The deluge can happen after my lifetime' is unfortunately one of the stronger views here.

In Jabiru however the world still seemed to be in order, attracting from all over the world, tourists, who gathered mainly in a few common places, leaving many places in Kakadu naturally unspoilt, which was good. The heat also played its role so that many people spent time with books and souvenirs in front of a cold drink rather than going out into 40 and above shade-temperature. The land and its heat is the essence of Kakadu. When adapting to it, nature's course here must be understood: 'Survival of only the fittest'. A short break at the visitors' centre gave us the energy to head back to a mighty rock formation, in the not too far distance.

NOURLANGI ROCK (BURRUNGUY)

Nourlangi Rock is probably the best known as well as one of the most important sites of Kakadu, including the 'Escarpment' and the surrounding lowlands of the vast Arnhem Land Plateau. This area is a unique part of Australia and indeed of the world. The imposing rock mass stood out in the dry grass and bushland plains. It has been greatly weathered, forming pillars and bridges; numerous walls have been undermined and have collapsed, forming shelters.

Escarpment - Kakadu, N. T.

The one along the base of the rock offers some of the finest indigenous art to be seen anywhere in the world. Boardwalks make a visit to the rock galleries easy and hopefully will keep people in the future away from these very old testimonies to early human cultural expressions - indeed the oldest known so far, dating back to 60 000 years.

Nourlangi rock art - Kakadu, N.T.

Nourlangi rock art - Kakadu, N.T.

There was not much protection in place for the artefacts; shelters were the only obvious protection against the extreme weather conditions. Trapped heat outside in the plain rose to well above 40 degrees Celsius in the shade: whereas in the shelters of the rock the temperature remained slightly more moderate. Aborigines say they have always been there; their ancestors - not mere physical forces - had created the area during a period of 'Dreamtime'. Scientists in recent times have established that this sandstone complex was laid down some 1600 million years ago after weathering of earlier formations. Early Aboriginal presence goes back in time to one of the Ice Ages, where the sea level was lower, allowing land bridges to connect with New Guinea.

The German explorer Ludwig Leichhardt was the first European to visit this region in 1845. Towards the end of an epic journey his exploration party disappeared dramatically in a way that to this day is unknown. How and where it happened are ongoing mysteries. Leichhardt reported in his journal about 'our good friends, the natives', whereas a later exploration of the area under the leadership of McKinley, sent by the

South Australian Government in 1865 to seek a new capital for their Northern Territory, contrasted with tales of an inhospitable country. One reason might have been the great differences between the dry and wet seasons and the explorers' abilities to deal with it.

At the southern end of the rock gallery, the path went up to a rock-neck delivering views along the Escarpment, a continuation of a large rock-face rising steeply above the adjacent plains. It is here where the inland sea stopped a long time ago. Today the plains are covered with a green carpet of eucalypt trees. The height of the plateau varies from 250 to 300 metres and in some places surpasses even 500 metres, indicating its original height. Nature shows here its ancient history, the oldest on earth and at the same time it shelters the oldest history of mankind.

Twin Falls - Kakadu, N.T.

Jim-Jim Falls - Kakadu, N.T.

Deep gorges can also be found on the plateau of the Escarpment, where the spectacular waterfalls of the 'Twin' and 'Jim-Jim Falls' have washed out a deep canyon. A massive watercourse drops onto the plateau during the wet season - first in a few steps before reaching the edge from where the water-masses tumble down filling the whole gorge with a mist. The falls are very difficult to access; no road goes there and on foot through the dense bushland, it could have been a dangerous undertaking, considering that the nearest point of the Kakadu Highway was 50 kilometres away. In Jabiru, helicopter services showed tourists this nature's spectacle from the air. Going back on the road towards Jabiru, we crossed the Arnhem Highway and followed the road into another area of interest.

UBIRR

Ubirr - Kakadu, N.T.

Again on wetland plains, massive weathered rock–islands and plateaus rose. In Ubirr Aboriginal artefacts decorate the walls of shelters, reflecting on the history and animal life of the area. These are located at the foot and top of a rock plateau, well protected from weather over thousands of years.

Rock art (sunrise) at Ubirr - Kakadu

Rock art at Ubirr - Kakadu

Despite the dry season, various shades of vivid green vegetation created a contrast to the bizarre rock formations on the plains. Another contrast appeared on the plateau - struggling yellow-brown grass, pandanus-spiralis and cabbage palms. With food, water and shelter in the area, Aborigines have had time to develop a rich and complex culture on the rock faces of the Ubirr site. There are few places in the world that offer such an easy life to a small indigenous population.

Ubirr – Kakadu, N.T.

Ubirr - Kakadu, N.T.

Visitors could enjoy walks along islands of rock walls. In between passages of grass and palm vegetation, they could reach the top of the plateau across stepped rock faces on a gradual climb. Views from there went far into the green wetlands, where darker green bushland took over in some places on the meadows.

Further to the east rose another rocky ridge adding to the special image of the area. The furthest eastern river-course of Kakadu, the East Alligator River, ran in the neighbourhood. Even in the dry season this river carried a lot of water from the Arnhem Land plateau to the sea. Its riverbanks were densely vegetated with mangroves, bush and trees, creating a perfect hideout on land for crocodiles.

Here on the lower part of the river course the salt-water crocodile could be expected. Thus, particular caution was required when walking in the area, because during early summer, not far from August, the crocs would come on to the land near the river and prepare a nest, piling it with leaves and branches in which to lay their eggs. From that moment, crocs become very vigilant and will aggressively fight any intruder. Make sure it's not you!

Our visit to Kakadu had now reached a turning point from where we could go back, not on the same road we came, but on the Kakadu Highway to the southwest. To call the two roads a highway into Kakadu was a bit of an overstatement. The top asphalt layer was in reasonable condition, but the width of the road didn't allow two wider vehicles to pass freely. Trucks from the Ranger Uranium Mine were on the road mainly during night. Generally it was a good praxis not to be on the road during night time.

Forests, bushland and river crossings changed from flat country to rocky hillsides, the closer we came to the Park's exit, near Pine Creek on the Stuart Highway. Most people must have chosen the Arnhem Highway for entrance and exit to Kakadu, while the alternate route remained without much traffic.

Turning Point

On our way we came across a roadhouse with the usual petrol pump station in front of it. It was off the road a little with the bush around it cleared away. The heat of the day impelled us to stop. The land in front of the hut raised a dust cloud; nobody else had arrived at the time. Not long after however, a seemingly brand new Toyota Landcruiser parked next to us. Out of it emerged a couple with a small girl, but none of them was the driver of the Landcruiser. A uniformed man occupied the driver's seat. His passengers were fashionably dressed in Safari uniforms. The husband called out in German when he set foot on the dusty ground, "We must have arrived at the end of the world."

He must have thought, when looking at this tiny set-up on the side of the road and having nothing else but Kakadu wilderness around, the end of the world must have looked like this. They must have been wealthy travellers - by the look of it having hired not only the car but also the driver for the Australian left-hand traffic. No luggage could be seen in the car. As it became apparent, the family came from Germany to collect their impressions from Kakadu and take them home in the most comfortable way possible. We kept to ourselves so they couldn't know that all their comments were understood by us.

Their arrogant appearance was not our 'beer'. They also produced a 'timetable' attitude when returning in a hurry to the car with a cup of coffee, including one for the driver and took off again, as if fleeing from the 'end of the world'. These people must have forgotten that they were not here on a business mission. However, it pays to remember that everybody has his own likes and dislikes.

Closer towards Pine Creek the area was again turned into ashes. Who had done it and whether it was really supposed to be a positive thing, became anybody's guess in the face of such devastation. It was hard to believe that out of these ashes stronger vegetation would be regenerated.

PINE CREEK

Pine Creek, a small hamlet on the Arnhem Land plateau, is located at a fairly high elevation. From there, the Stuart Highway goes constantly downhill towards Darwin. Around Christmas time in the middle of the summer heat-hell, a bicycle race usually takes place, and to make it tough enough, it starts in Darwin going all the way uphill to Pine Creek over a distance of 200 kilometres. My previous employer in Brisbane had lived a number of years in Darwin. He participated in this gruelling race, which probably made him the tough man he was and still is. Our tour circuit through the Top End finished for us in Pine Creek.

TERMITE MOUND COUNTRY

During this part of our tour we came across two remarkable termite mound sites. These are a well-established element of Northern Australia. Here termite populations have built the highest termite mounds in the world, which again is a direct indication of the hot climate in the Top End. Before leaving the area, I want to revisit the two places of special termite interest - Litchfield National Park and near the Kakadu Wetlands.

In Litchfield we found a 6-metre high termite mound. Also in Litchfield, in a small wetland area, plank walkways above ground led close to a colony of mounds, which rose out of the wet ground in a flat shape on a wide base, pronged at the top. They were 'Magnetic Termite Mounds' found nowhere else in the world. Termite mounds are always cleared and clean around their wider base, a result of the termites' activity to remove all biological material from the ground.

The white ants or termites are clever builders, having invented long before us their air-conditioned housing. They live underground, whereas the mound above contains sophisticated tunnels changing in size from the bottom to the top, from larger to smaller, in order to achieve a natural compression of the hot air. A gradual decompression sends small amounts of cooler air downwards inside the mound, constantly making the 'air conditioning' work. When looking at a termite mound, it is worth remembering, the white ants don't live in it but there are other creatures sharing the cooler conditions of an inner termite mound – the snakes. They won't bother the termites, but are certainly a curious intruder. Never try to put a hand into a tunnel of a termite mound! The snake surprise could end up deadly.

Unique Magnetic Termite Mounds – Northern Territory

Arja beside a termite mound - Kakadu, N.T.

The other termite mound place in Kakadu near its western entrance to Arnhem Highway was interesting in as much as the mounds congregated in one place like a colony. Mounds also rose there to heights of several metres, shaped into solid irregular cones. Looking at them close up didn't reveal any white ant life. Were there ants in these fortresses? Ants are highly organized and remain in their underground housing fulfilling various tasks like composting organic materials for their food intake preparation. Bacteria break down cellulose in a form of sugar on which the ants feed. Working ants clean the 'housing estate' of waste, whereas soldier ants are on guard, not always visible to us, but reporting what is happening around their ant world. In the underground they have a section dedicated to a nursery, where the young are raised - fed, cleaned and patiently taught ant lessons preparing them for an ant community task from an early age.

The presence of onlookers in the mound area kept the ants in hiding. I left however a piece of bread on the ground near a mound, walked away for a few minutes and returned to watch the ants starting to move the bread slice underground bit by bit near the mound. Ants are extremely alert and efficient because of a team presence, in which tasks are collectively solved. I often found it worthwhile in my life to observe an anthill and how these active creatures are organized. To do so, time is an important factor, because ants react to a foreign presence and do not show their standard life patterns unless you can wait until the ants have settled back into their routines.

SOUTHBOUND

I leave here our excursion into the ant world to focus on our return tour to Queensland. We had arrived in Pine Creek. On the outskirts of this settlement a picnic place invited us to stop at the table and benches around. Gale winds blew from the south, dropping the temperature here dramatically from that in Kakadu; surprises on an Australian tour are always guaranteed.

LARRIMAH

120 kilometres further south in the Katherine Gorge the temperature was back to 'normal'. The road in front of us was familiar but with that interesting difference that travelling in an opposite direction often makes. At the end of another driving day we stopped at Larrimah, a place with two caravan parks and a few more houses along the eastern side of the Stuart Highway. In 1983, 18 years earlier, we came through here from Western Australia. This time we looked in vain for the prize winning park set-up with its magnificent deep red bougainvillea over its entrance. Nothing of this successful transformation of an arid land into a flourishing oasis could be seen any more; the place was left in a deplorable state. One generation's effort didn't unfortunately secure the next generation's efforts.

The other caravan park further down the road had its gates open, prompting us to enter and stay overnight. Smouldering ashes under rows of bush sent smoke everywhere to keep mosquitos out of the place, though getting rid of one problem caused another one. Only one spot in the back of the park was not engulfed by the fiery smoke. This was where there was a pond. We soon found out that when the water in it next to our resting place noisily splashed, a monstrous crocodile appeared. The fence between helped us to retain our confidence to stay where we were.

After having introduced itself, the croc moved slowly back into the pond keeping the nostrils and the eyes just above the water. The tail on the ground kept the croc floating under the surface. People here had a fully-grown saltwater crocodile of 4.5 metres as their pet, something not commonly found elsewhere. At night I couldn't help but check on the croc to see what it was doing. In the moonshine out of the night's sky the eyes of the croc appeared as two red points in the water. Lying motionless under the surface, only the dark shade of its body could be seen. As the croc made no attempt to move, I could be assured and go back to sleep. Was the croc watching the moon?

Up until first daylight the next morning the croc had remained in exactly the same position, demonstrating that it had all the time in the world to wait. For what, soon became clear, when the owner of the park arrived with one slaughtered chicken, throwing it over the fence. The calm in the pond was shattered as, with incredible strength and speed, the croc was out of the water grabbing the chicken with its jaws. It shook its head, vehemently reducing the chicken's body and returned with the prey slowly into the pond. While the croc returned to the pond with its prey we were in the neighbourhood. A couple of bites were enough to make the prey disappear between the jaws. Calm resumed; the croc waited again under the surface. This spectacle was already worth our stay in the caravan park.

Next to the log barrier a strongly built buffalo grazed on dry grassland under scattered eucalypt trees outside the caravan park. Heavy horns kept its head in the grass until I decided to take a shot with my camera from close range. The flash of the camera however took the buffalo by surprise so that the animal's heavy body suddenly jumped up into the air, all four legs becoming airborne; dust and stone from the hoofs flew straight towards me, causing me a lot of trouble to save my camera and myself from this onslaught of dirt - the result: no photo.

Even with the rising sun the temperature again turned rather cool after leaving the Top End of the Northern Territory. The toll-bar at the caravan park's entrance was kept closed during the night. As we were the only guests, the owner gave us the key to unlock the bar across the driveway and told us to close it again and leave the key in the mailbox of the main building. Nobody wanted to be up early in the morning when we left.

Only a short time later, bushfires crossing the road again forced us to stop at a safe distance and wait until a passage through was found. In the air behind the flames and the smoke-clouds, wedge-tailed eagles circled looking for grilled wildlife.

Burning bush - Northern Territory

The devastation by fire in this arid stony land was shocking. By burning the land there was not only a focus on regeneration of the flora as I mentioned previously, but also a traditional way of an easier hunting practice by Aborigines, especially in the past. Today it looks like this has become a tradition without proper further considerations of the impact of such actions. Here we had a case of 'habitual-right' versus rational understanding. A tradition, which turns questionable, always takes time to correct; it is most definitely the case here.

THE THREE WAYS

A sudden drop in temperature on the Barkley Highway east of Three Ways, prompted us to continue without stopping on this leg through isolated countryside, where hardly a car passed us during a one-hour drive. In some places dry grass stood to man's height on both sides of the road. Along a two-metre strip, which followed the sides of the road, the grass was cut short avoiding the starting of fire by carelessly throwing cigarettes out of a car. Despite this there was still somebody next to the high dry grass maintaining an open fire, probably to keep warm. The fire catching the grass would have started an inferno. Negligence of people is often a trigger for the many fires in Australia. Fire is final and it should be avoided whenever possible. The area could be called, 'Land of many stones, less bread.'

EASTBOUND TO QUEENSLAND

CAMOOWEAL

Border crossing

Where the good road stopped, Queensland added again more flora to the land starting with bush, followed by eucalypt trees and closer to the coast, dense forests covered the mountains of the Great Dividing Ranges. A journey of nature's surprises lay ahead.

Arriving late just before sunset in Queensland's border town of Camooweal, we were lucky to squeeze into its caravan park for the night. In the furthest corner of the park under a large acacia tree was the only spot left. I convinced the owner to give us a permit to stay. Initially we were told there was no room left. Our previous knowledge of the place told us however that under the acacia tree was a hidden space, in our view the best place anyway, the only one with a bit of a privacy.

To get into the spot with our car, a campervan had to first be moved out of the way. The couple with their two young sons spoke to us in English, but to each other in German. As we responded in German their surprise was instant. The German couple's reaction turned out to be rather cautious, watching us for a while from a distance as we probably did to them. A breakthrough however didn't take long and Nicky and Rainer came towards us suggesting, "When our boys are in bed, we could have a bottle of good Australian wine together. What do you think?"

"No problem – we'll put some crackers and cheese on the table and our party can take off."

"We can also bring the glasses for the wine."

"This turns our party into a five-star event; see you then."

The couple that were originally from Germany have lived for a number of years in Hong Kong, escaping to Australia on a holiday from the city's 'concrete jungle'. Nicky had this to say, "It's so rewarding for a change to see 'nothing' for long distances here in Australia and not to have the ever-dominant view of Hong Kong's towers."

People living outside their traditional area mostly adopt more cautious views, simply because they know more. People have knowledge and the more people we know, the more we can learn in real terms. Such learning processes never end as long as we live, contrary to formal learning, in which an end result is 'cemented'. Documented in black and white, it is safe enough to carry home. Our conversation accompanied by wine, cheese, olives, and crackers lasted well into the cooler hours of the early morning.

"We were sent by the German Government to Hong Kong to assist in the education of our citizens, who work for German companies in China. Life in Hong Kong is very different from that in Germany; we learn about the people, their culture, and their country. Our children can only benefit from it for their own future. At present the employment situation in Germany is like this: if you want to keep your job, you have to be flexible and accept a transfer to another country. Thus, the future might become that not only goods are internationally exchanged, but people with their know-how as well. We love the colourful societies in Asia; we would personally however like to live in Australia, a country with plenty of wide-open spaces. Since we left Adelaide, we had not seen one cloud on our tour through Australia; you are spoilt here with the weather. And on the road we eventually saw one other car about once an hour. There must be opportunities in abundance in this country. What is your experience since you arrived?"

"Money doesn't grow on trees here just to be picked; there is really no single recipe of how to succeed in Australia. With time and perseverance everybody can make it in Australia just like everywhere else in the world. It all depends where your priorities are. You have seen the outback and you should have a good idea about what it means here to make ends meet. We have made it in Australia, but it didn't happen overnight. Our road was also bumpy, especially in the beginning."

None of us realised how quickly time had passed, as both parties exchanged many of their experiences from around the world and also from Germany. Outside Germany we have quietly changed our views and only when returning will we recognise these changes. Many little occurrences in daily life lead usually to a bigger picture and if brought up in a conversation with others, it opens a wider understanding, but only, when everybody participates from wide experience. People that travel have more to tell than the ones that don't. Some confirmations richer, our parties sought that bit of sleep for the remaining few hours of the night, ready for another day's travel.

With sunrise we were back on the road, leaving a farewell note at the campervan door of our friendly neighbours. As we headed to the east, the blinding sun stood in front of us. The partly bitumen and dusty stone road required a slow speed at this time and caution in the case of oncoming traffic. An approaching dust-cloud took up most of our vision and in some cases threw up stones, which could easily cause a breakage when hitting a car window.

In 1983 I lost a windscreen on this route from a stone of a careless, oncoming fast vehicle. This time our caution paid off; we didn't want to drive again all the way to Mount Isa without a windscreen, which could only be described as an unpleasant experience. In such a case one can drive only very slowly and must stop each time on the side of the road in the event of an oncoming or overtaking car. The missing windscreen would otherwise allow in stones and dust from the road. Flies in their millions in the air made life difficult enough already. It could only be wished that more people had experienced a broken windscreen on an outback road and I bet in that case, far fewer incidents would occur. Leaving Mount

Isa behind, the road improved instantly as we had come back to the rich mining businesses of Mount Isa, which ensured a better road.

CLONCURRY AND THE ROYAL FLYING DOCTOR SERVICE

Rugged mountain areas along a winding road came to an end in Cloncurry. It was here that we had arrived a couple of weeks earlier from the south on the Matilda Highway on 'the road to Nitmiluk'. 'Mary Kathleen Memorial Park' on the outskirts of the small town received a visit from us. On our first visit I didn't mention the Park's name.

The outback town of Cloncurry is the birthplace of John Flynn, the founder of the Royal Flying Doctor Service, a real Australian pioneering idea initiated in 1928 and still operating today across the entire Australian outback. In the outback, the R.F.D.S. deserves mention mostly because of the people behind it. Since the time of Mary Kathleen, many more courageous men and women with aircrafts have answered countless calls from people in need over an area comparable to the size of most of Europe.

Sacrifices and untold heroic actions are the legacies of this Australian institution, unique in the world. Doctors, nurses and pilots of the Royal Flying Doctor Service deserve the nation's utmost respect, because they are doing more than just a job, being committed to helping those in need, regardless of time, distance and whoever might be in need. A call for them has always been a serious one; no one would call because of a common cold.

I can still remember a report in the 1980's from South Australia, when a farmer fell off his tractor and the ploughing machine kept moving, cutting off one of the farmer's legs. Despite his severe condition, the farmer reached the tractor with the cut leg and drove some distance to get help. The Flying Doctor Service arrived and saved his leg and his life. With such determination on both sides, help can often succeed.

An equally outstanding Australian icon would be the Outback Radio School, an institution operating already for over 100 years. Especially talented teachers serve children in remote areas of the outback, teaching them subjects in a unique way. Each teacher-student relationship over the radio is without doubt a special experience with its own story. A lack of direct contact is compensated by special relationships, which are developed on both sides to support an understanding: a gift that can work very positively in a student's future life.

8 times more square miles than people

The road now went from flat country straight to the horizon. Places like Julia Creek had a sign at the entrance telling the number of residents, the size of the area and the main commercial activity, like cattle and wheat farming. In Cloncurry and Julia Creek the number of square miles outnumbered the residents considerably. Huge properties could be found again. Parallel to the road, big concrete power poles lined up in even distances, whereas on the opposite side ran an embankment, which connected Mount Isa to the coast by rail.

RICHMOND

Wide farming land continued all the way to Richmond. On a ridge slightly higher than the surrounding countryside, the town unfolded on both sides of a main road with a well-landscaped centre-area of fresh green lawns and pockets of flowers.

Richmond pub and dinosaur - Queensland

A beautiful Queensland pub with its typical all-round-veranda and large high roofing was located in the town centre. At the intersection in front of the pub a life-sized dinosaur replica showed proudly the importance of the area within the history of the dinosaur. A modern building in the neighbourhood exhibited dinosaur discoveries of the area; according to current knowledge they are the oldest ones.

Outside the town the land dropped sharply in the north to a lower region. First, eucalypt forests appeared in the east. The country didn't look bone dry any more; it was coping better with the dry season of winter. On the ridge to the southeast serious fossil hunters could have made their own discoveries, as the area was not closed off to the public at that time. Richmond as a whole presented itself as a well-developed town. Was this because of the dinosaur-discovery attracting numbers of visitors during the year or the rich farming area or both? The caravan park at the eastern end of the town surprised visitors with its clean modern layout.

When first looking around the place, we found ourselves in trouble with the proud owner. "Can't you see us first like everybody else does and not enter before you have our permission?" Apologizing for our curiosity and adding our written praise of the place in the comment section of the bookings page, quickly turned discord into friendly acceptance. The rest of our stay went well in a friendly atmosphere - 'a hard shell often has a softer core' described the park's owners perfectly.

Near the park in the centre of the road was a stagecoach from the past on display. It looked like new and was protected fully around. The workmanship of this exhibit truly indicated the importance of delivering post in the outback.

Historic mail coach — Richmond, Queensland

After a silent clear outback night, stars were the only signposts into the unlimited universe. Our day started early again. Kangaroos turned up near the road, demanding driving caution. Grassland and the start of eucalypt forests provided food and shelter for wildlife, pushing the outback slowly back.

As we rolled into Hughenden, no people could be seen; night hadn't fully passed yet. Flocks of galahs in their thousands occupied the main road's power lines, screeching their morning messages so loudly that one couldn't hear one's own voice. The telephone box on the side of the road couldn't overcome this noise so that we had to abandon our call home. The galahs had their say at the start of a new day, calling all their 'mates' to visit the crops on the farmland for the rest of the day.

Galah flocks - Hughenden, Queensland

Farmers had not much choice but to leave a share of the crop to the wildlife. The galahs made their point clear from high up on the power lines, while we continued on the road further east. People of Hughenden might have started the day possibly after the galah flocks had moved out of town. Were the birds a wake-up call for the town?

TORRENS CREEK

Torrens Creek, a hamlet on the road, invited us to stop. The first thing that caught our eye were the mango trees, a sign that coastal moisture has already reached this area, because mango trees need humid conditions during summer for new growth, flowers and fruit. When matured, the trees are drought resistant as long as they receive their bit of 'mango madness' just like the hot and humid climate conditions of the Northern Territory.

A solid timber table and benches, one on each long side, became a perfect opportunity to have our breakfast. We were not alone for long; cheeky black-brown birds arrived on the table competing with us for our wheat biscuits and breadcrumbs. Not stopping at the crumbs, they also stole directly from the bowl and even followed the spoon from plate to mouth. This was something new that we had never experienced before. The birds had no fear, no 'manners'. In some instances we could have easily grabbed a bird, but we distanced ourselves and tried to enjoy these rebellious residents of Torrens Creek. However it meant that we really couldn't enjoy our breakfast. When everything was off the table, the birds moved into the mango trees behind us, planning their next move.

The picnic place also had a memorial stone. As the birds retreated, we were able to get a closer look at the stone, which showed that the residents of Torrens Creek have commemorated one of their own citizens from the late 19th century, who had lived here uninterrupted for 30 years at the doorstep of the outback and led an 'honest life'. At that time, a resident's character and perseverance were honoured, for the pursuit of conquering the outback step by step. Steadfast local residents formed the backbone in times without a road, power, telephone, railway, and certainly no car. I haven't seen such recognition elsewhere in the world. During that earlier time, every individual embodied a particular importance with others in the quest for survival.

'The steps to the outback' also included the coastal fringes with the Great Dividing Ranges not far away. Mountain ranges completely covered with a green forest-carpet showed up on the horizon. After 8600 kilometres on 'the road to Nitmiluk', North Queensland was to become a new chapter of our tour.

Welcome to the Range

Great Dividing Range - North Queensland

NORTH QUEENSLAND

The dry image of the outback changed dramatically; nature's Eden must have started here. Mountains of the Seventy Mile Range rose sharply, uninterrupted by dense forests and pointing into the sky. Dominant red-yellow-brown colours in the outback changed in the Dividing Ranges into exclusively green shades. Kangaroos had plenty on which to feed in this vast area and didn't present a risk on the road any more.

CHARTERS TOWERS

Charters Towers is a charming little town not far from Townsville. Queenslander colonial-style buildings around the town centre looked back more than 100 years to a gold-rush time. This time had seen many pioneers making their fortune and this was still reflected today in the town's image. Losses of that time haven't left visible traces although they were certainly not insignificant.

Charters Towers - North Queensland

The Town Hall is especially well laid out, as are the two pubs, each in a different location. Numerous tall palms gave the first impressions of a tropical environment. The eastern outskirts introduced a traveller into lush tropical gardens on perfect green lawns of the coastal region.

TOWNSVILLE

Towards Townsville - North Queensland

Traffic towards Townsville increased constantly and when the mountains receded, Townsville lay on a coastal plain along a wide bow of a Pacific Ocean bay. One rocky hill, named Castle Hill, holds its ground virtually in the centre of the rapidly growing city. Out in the bay, Magnetic Island rises magnificently out of the ocean. Townsville enjoys a privileged position, surrounded by mountains, rainforests and sea. The town with its 80 000 residents in 2001 was not really a big place yet. However development trends showed a steep increase. Townsville wanted to remain the capital of North Queensland.

Family bonds called for a break here from our Nitmiluk expedition. Our eldest son Risto lived with his wife in this tropical oasis. Their home on a big block of land in the city near the Ross River received constant improvements over time, making their dream home come true in the strong tradition of migrants. Keriann, a fifth generation Aussie, gives her migrant husband a supportive hand in all work on the property; this way they can both enjoy the personal progress in their lives. For town living, the area was special, located in a cul de sac.

From the high veranda around the house, big mango and Poinciana trees in the neighbourhood hindered the view to the city, taking it further to Castle Hill. The garden and swimming pool contributed to their pride in their own home. Two German shepherds extended the family tradition also in Townsville adding to a happy and secure lifestyle with their presence. The Aussie dream of owning your own home has already started to be out of reach for many. Grabbing opportunities at the right time in life is very much linked to luck. The plan for this part of our journey was that all four of us explore Townsville first and then gradually we would move further afield relying on the local experience of our younger generation.

Home of eldest son, Risto, in Townsville - North Queensland

Focussing on Townsville, a trip up to Castle Hill is a must to gain a general view over the city and its surroundings. The residential district stopped at the foothills but the road went steeply around the rocky hill continuing right to the top. Joggers on the road had to be watched carefully as we drove to the top. The Pacific hillside rose in barren rock, whereas on the opposite inland side scattered bush and eucalypt trees were more dominant.

An area at the top allowed parking and there was a small fenced lookout platform at the end of a long, stepped path. Superb views unfolded over the entire city. Around the rocky hill, forest-covered mountains closed in the plain to the west. Towards the south rose Mount Stuart, considerably higher than Castle Hill. Townsville's beach-promenade with its stretch of sandy beach, extensive landscaping of tropical gardens, and pavements and streets along the coastline, followed the bay line.

Protected seawater pools on the beach reminded of the danger from sea creatures, especially here in North Queensland. No one should ever attempt to swim in a non-protected beach area. There are many deadly creatures: box jellyfish, sharks, stingray, sea snakes, stonefish etc. The

Pacific bay lay calm; its surface glittered the more the eye followed the horizon. Like a colossus in the sea, Magnetic Island sheltered the bay partly from the open sea. Green vegetation with the exemption of a few rock cliffs marked the island rather darkly. To complete the panoramic view from Mount Stuart, the runway of Townsville's airport could be seen in the north, way out from housing estates. There was another scenic opportunity at night with only city lights sparkling from beneath and stars from above, unveiling shades and vague contours.

Returning, the steep descent to the city required caution not to go too fast, because there was nothing here to stop somebody from tumbling quickly down the rock faces instead of remaining on the road. Mount Stuart in the south is much higher than Castle Hill, offering even greater views from its peak. The road wound in steep serpentines all the way up between scattered eucalypt trees. Rocky slopes allowed the trees to grow only very slowly making the Stuart Oak a special species; it is known for its extremely hard timber. An aerial installation on top of Mount Stuart served the air traffic control ensuring that aircrafts to and from Townsville found their way safely through the mountains.

In Townsville the Maritime Museum could not be missed, a comprehensive exhibition of the Pacific's sea-life – well worth a visit. In its modern buildings a full-sized sailing ship including hull, masts and sails was constructed through the floor levels.

Massive timber sections and an astonishing workmanship told of a pioneering past.

For somebody who likes shopping, the city centre was a no-traffic zone and when packed on Sunday mornings with little market stalls, spread across the road attracting crowds of people.

MAGNETIC ISLAND

Our tourist program also included moving away from the city, across the bay to Magnetic Island. There was a regular boat service connecting the island to the mainland. As our son had his own boat however, we went independently across to the island. The passage didn't take more than half an hour at a good speed. A footbridge into the sea made anchoring our boat easy in the small bay, which on both its ends had massive rock formations protecting the bay from the wider, open waters. Looking back in the direction from where we came, only Castle Hill stuck out on the plain and in the background mountains surrounded it in a wide semi-circle.

Walking straight from a narrow stony beach onto the land of Magnetic Island, we first saw tall coconut trees forming a small forest. Baskets on the ground held coconuts free to take, because they were in abundance here. Visitors needed to be very cautious when walking under the coconut trees. A coconut falling from high up could have a devastating impact when hitting somebody. Cutting a hard coconut shell with a machete without incurring an injury requires skilful handling. Coconut milk and the sweet flesh are 'paradise food' quickly satisfying any hunger and thirst, especially when the coconuts are free.

Besides the usual tourist facilities, there was also a rental-place for go-cart-like vehicles, which could be used to move around the island's roads. None was available at our arrival; therefore we explored part of the island on foot. Not far away there was a housing estate, where people who could afford an island-life lived, away from the city's hectic life.

Climbing the rocks in the northern end of the bay, gave us a panoramic view across the island and back to the mainland. Everything appeared on such a grand scale here. The ocean bay and the distant mainland with its mountains appeared less dominating; the sky reached to the horizon all around. The sea in the bay below lay totally still in the lee of the island, whereas coastlines to the open Pacific showed, even from the distance, white caps of mighty waves. Dense bushland covered most of the island and few hills rose above the rest of the land.

An island holiday was certainly tempting, only if the cost of living and all the charges around were more tailored for the average person's wallet. A holiday on Magnetic Island was not on our minds however; there were enough other people interested instead of us. Our planned overall time on 'the road to Nitmiluk' allowed us time to travel further north into a tropical paradise not found elsewhere in Australia and hardly anywhere else in the world.

This leg of our tour became a contrast to the previous 'road to Nitmiluk': rainforest-covered mountains reached beachfronts and out in the Pacific Ocean lay many islands supporting the World Heritage listed Great Barrier Reef. Even the small towns haven't changed the natural beauty of North Queensland yet. When talking about the tropics, Australia is the only part in the tropical regions of the world that, because of its isolation, is free of diseases, a merit that visiting tourists in the area shouldn't underestimate. Not far away, just across Torres Strait further north, Papua New Guinea lies and here tropical drawbacks are still prevalent.

NORTHBOUND

Going north from Townsville, the road always followed the coast, where sugarcane fields stood dense and well over man's height in the coastal plains between the sea and mountains. A small railway line passed occasionally in front of cane fields, transporting the harvest in fenced box-train carriages with a steam engine in front. It was bound for the sugar mill further north in Tully.

On the road to Tully, accompanied by sugar-cane
fields on both sides - North Queensland

Before arriving in Tully, the road climbed past Ingham up into a coastal mountain range just opposite Hinchinbrook Island. An ocean channel separates the island from the mainland. Misty clouds kept hiding the peaks of massive mountain colossi, also covered completely with a variety of rainforest greens. The island's natural varieties included fragile heath-vegetation, patches of lush rainforest and extensive eucalypt forests descending to a mangrove-fringed channel in the west and sweeping bays and rocky headlands along the east coast.

A visit to the island required a permit needed for all camping, including walking the Thorsborne Trail: a 32 kilometre trail along Hinchinbrook's east coast named after the late Arthur Thorsborne who, with his wife Margaret, had a lifelong interest in nature conservation. This included monitoring of Torresian imperial pigeons, which migrate to nest on local islands in summer. The trail was not a graded or hardened walking track and in some areas was rough and difficult to traverse. Restricting numbers of bushwalkers helped minimise the environmental impact and maintain the wilderness setting.

After the Lookout on the mainland, the road descended to Cardwell into plains of sugarcane fields. This area has one of the highest rainfalls in the world. Numerous waterfalls in the mountains add to the rich tropical image of the area; Jourama, Wallaman, and Murray Falls could all be reached from the coast within three driving hours inland. Heading for a waterfall through silent mountainous rainforests was like a pilgrimage to nature's 'cathedral'.

As we arrived in Tully, the central mill location of the sugarcane area, it lived up to its reputation – 'it rains every day in Tully'. In fact, it was the first brief shower we had experienced on the whole Nitmiluk trip. The mill-complex in Tully with its smoking chimneys made up most of the town's image. What surprised us was the fact that here in the tropics, migrants from Finland also lived. They had even established their own Finnish Club. A bigger contrast between the cold Finland and the tropical Tully could hardly be imagined. There is a thesis that mankind originates from the tropics and had migrated only under nature's pressure into colder zones. Is the Finnish migration also a return to the grass roots?

Life in a hot-warm climate can have a longer span than in the cold climate - when enough attention is given to health issues - because the blood in a hot climate becomes thinner and therefore supports a heart in working more easily. A health problem in a hot climate however can have more far-reaching consequences than in a cold climate. To balance awareness between health and the climate is obviously the best answer.

In Innisfail another sudden brief shower in the middle of the day helped to wash off the dust from the Outback. Sunshine returned straight after, turning the air humid even during the dry winter season. The town was a first-rate tourist Mecca; information for places of interest was available everywhere. A sign in the middle of the main road stood 8 metres high, indicating that this was the annual rainfall of Innisfail.

To my knowledge, only the volcano-centre of the island Kauai in Hawaii has more precipitation during a year.

The road went steeply inland from Innisfail up to mountain passes before entering the Atherton Tablelands. In the foothills, vigorously grown banana trees could be seen in vast plantations and on the mountain slopes coffee and tea took over. The volcanic soils and ample rainfall in the area provide the perfect conditions in which to grow quality tea that rivals the best in the world.

TEA PLANTATION VISIT

In the Nerada Valley we visited a model tea plantation, where guests could find accommodation while tasting the farm's tea. They also got a good picture of the amount of work going into hand-picking of young, fresh tea leaves every two to four weeks throughout the year, plus processing for fresh deliveries to the consumer.

From a distance, tea and coffee bushes don't look much different from each other. Both have dense dark-green leaves, but coffee was found more in the higher region of the Tablelands. A day as a guest on a tea-farm surrounded by mountains and rainforests was a memorable experience. The owner, Dr Alan Maruff migrated from India in the early 1950's and settled in the township of Innisfail. He recognised the potential for growing tea in the area when he and his wife observed how similar the surrounding landscape was to some of the famous tea growing regions of Northern India. In 1958 he purchased the land in Nerada Valley and commenced tea planting, which marked the beginning of Nerada tea.

The mountain pass reached the clouds in the rainforest causing the temperature to drop significantly. A rest place off the road in a forest clearing became the perfect opportunity to start a decent picnic at an open barbecue area. The whole place was drenched with humidity so that starting a fire became quite a task with only wet branches on the ground; dead grass was one option to get the fire started.

Family picnic at Crawford Lookout - North Queensland

Tourists we had met on the coast didn't make it there that day, so we were on our own. A short walking distance away from the road a forest corridor, called Crawford Lookout, opened onto views into a deep rocky gully, where only a little water fell down, disappearing from sight over sharp, stepped rock-edges. To the north, past an almost vertical forest edge of a neighbouring mountain, the eye caught a window view into sweeping green coastal sugarcane fields.

ATHERTON TABLELANDS

Back on the road and travelling further west towards the Atherton Tablelands, dense retreating forests left the misty clouds behind, granting lush green meadows more and more space. Milla–Milla Falls in a closed forest area took water down to the coast in creeks and rivers from this wet area. Many other waterfalls followed the same pattern: Mungalli, Souita, Pekina, Millstream, Zillie, Dinner, and Malanda Falls. West of the coastal mountain ridge, the humidity and rainfall from rising clouds gradually diminished and, further inland, turned into drier outback conditions.

Rainforest - North Queensland

Heading north towards Malanda and Yungaburra, farmland of sugar cane and wheat and maize was introduced; standing high, it would soon deliver a rich harvest. Malanda was the centre of the only dairy industry in the tropics, distributing milk on 'the Longest Milk-Run of the World'- Townsville, Alice Springs, Darwin, Papua New Guinea and South-East Asia.

Settlements on the Tablelands didn't appear large yet; only small housing estates made up Yungaburra. Just outside the town, a huge Curtain Fig Tree attracted our attention. It was the Tableland's most famous tree, a gigantic spreading tangle of aerial roots created by the fig strangling the original host tree and taking over. The tree is native to North Queensland.

Curtain Fig Tree - Atherton Tablelands, North Queensland

Still in Yungaburra, a Swiss family had created their own Switzerland with a restaurant linking their service to a Swiss-tradition in food, music and style, not forgetting the 'Swiss-prices'. The green countryside did match their Swiss idea; only the rugged Swiss mountains were missing. These were replaced here by the more gentle hillsides of the lush Atherton Tablelands. The coastal mountains were however not far away. In many parts of the world, where mountains dominate a landscape, Swiss citizens can be found, recreating their small Switzerland away from 'home'.

Lake Tinaroo - Atherton Tablelands, North Queensland

The vicinity of Lake Tinaroo gave numbers of visitors sporting opportunities along the shores of this freshwater lake. Atherton was the centre of the shire of the same name, administrating its commercial activities - mainly rich farming land plus increasingly attracting tourism from the coast especially on its balmy summer days without the oppressive coastal mugginess. All standards of accommodation and hospitality could be found in this modern agricultural town-centre. As the 11th of August was a special event on our family calendar -33 years earlier we had 'tied the knot' in Finland - it gave us a good excuse to celebrate in style with a luxurious meal and excellent Australian wine on an outdoor veranda of a local restaurant in Atherton.

A beautifully restored 1920's steam train also took us on board the next day starting from the outskirts of the town and travelling into the rocky hills of Herberton through agricultural land and forests on one of Queensland's steepest railway lines. Here the country didn't compete with front-running technology, but maintained some of its heritage, offering people its tradition.

A journey on an old steam train remains a special experience, despite the pull of modern technology. The smell of a puffing engine and the pulsing speed gives enough time for observations into the environment either from curtained carriage windows or from open carriages, where passengers could choose between more or less fresh air on either hard wooden benches or comfortable cushioned seats. The train journey also went past Carrington Falls and when rounding a bend we came in view of the curtain of water tumbling down rocky cliffs and refreshing the air in a surrounding rainforest pocket.

Other destinations of interest in the area were further north in Mareeba. Atherton Shire owed its existence to 'red gold'- the red cedar tree, which grew abundantly in the dense rainforests of the Tablelands. Today, maize, peanuts, potatoes, tropical fruit, and sugarcane thrive in the rich red volcanic soil. The town of Mareeba also has a rich history of gold mining dating back to 1876. The specialized farming in the area also included coffee.

COFFEE WORKS VISIT

Coffee plantation - Atherton Tablelands

We visited the coffee plantation outside the town, where rows of coffee bushes were precisely planted. The bushes were flowering at the time with bright white stellar-blossoms in a row on both sides of each branch. Mareeba 'Coffee Works' demonstrated in its small modern plant, what coffee varieties it could produce locally. A tasting tour through the Coffee Works was on offer for a fee, reinforcing the idea that 'nothing in this world is free.'

Small spaces between the processing equipment, which tumbled, washed, dried, sorted, roasted and packed, allowed better supervision of the process with a minimum of staff. The works ran 7 days a week and was proudly family-owned and operated, something to be especially proud of in a world increasingly dominated by large business. The pride came though at a price: seven-days-a-week work. That's probably why the name 'Coffee Works' had been chosen.

Anyone who had an interest in mining history could visit Tyrconnell's historic mine-site. The 120-year-old ten-head stamping battery could be stirred into action, giving a real sense of the pioneers at work. To round off our visit to Mareeba, we went northwest, to the Mareeba Wetlands. A sense of endurance was needed to walk the track along fields to reach the wetland's lake before being asked to pay a high entrance fee for looking at bird life that may or may not turn up. We couldn't be impressed on that day and rather gave others the opportunity to wait and see what happens. At home in Southeast Queensland, we were probably a bit spoilt having a Natural Park, a lagoon and wild bird life in our own backyard. The ones without this privilege might, with time and patience, see something in these wetlands.

MANGO WINERY VISIT

Mango Winery at Mareeba - Atherton Tablelands

As we returned from the Wetland excursion back onto the main road leading into Mareeba, a road branched off on the opposite side. A mango farm was located further inland along Bilwon Road, worthwhile paying a visit. It was still early in the morning and nobody could be seen in the centre of the property around the buildings.

In perfectly geometric positions stood the mango trees; they all looked the same in size and the land was free of weeds and very clean as if a machine had just cleaned the whole area. As we stood in front of the domestic building, a lady whom we addressed came out.

"We are a bit early for a Sunday and hope you don't mind us having a look at your fantastic farm."

"You are not early; we are just having our morning break. Our day started much earlier. My husband will be with you in a few moments; let him have his cup of coffee first. Meanwhile you are welcome to look around, but stay out of the bottom building for the time being."

Not much later the farmer turned up, "You are earlier than others. Do you want me to show you around?"

"If you have the time, we would love to join you."

The farmer started his long story. "We migrated from Italy 25 years ago and five years later bought this farm in a completely run down state. The owners at the time alleged there was no money in mangoes. My whole family, including the children, took on the challenge of this place. First, all the existing trees, which had not been looked after, were pulled out, and we systematically replanted our own Australian variety - the Kensington Red mango. As you can see, they have grown well since.

With our own specially built machine we prune the trees every year. We drive along the trees and cut them back with the big self-made hedge-scissors, leaving a virtually square layout after going along in all four directions. Mango trees love pruning and subsequently produce bigger fruit in the new season. When the fruit is ready to be picked in November, we have developed a method to make wine out of our mangoes, which is far more difficult than from grapes. This way we don't have the worries of transporting the mangoes to distant markets to sell.

We sell our wine today only to orders from around the world. Come and have a look for yourself at my processing plant, where you can taste my three mango wine varieties. When you buy wine, the taste is free; otherwise I'll charge two dollars for each person. As you can see, there is a lot of money invested in these installations; everything had to be built out of stainless steel to deal with the mangoes. Today we are proud to own everything; our family has worked hard all those years. We are well off, because our idea not to sell only the fruit, but to make wine out of it has finally paid off. We sell two different bottle-sizes of three varieties: 'dry' is like a wine, 'medium' is softer on the palate with a stronger hint of fruit and 'sweet' is very smooth and has a rich undertone of fruit. All three have a rich flavour only Kensington mangoes can supply. We have to keep the whole process of making mango wine to ourselves because we don't want to increase competition by telling people about the process.

There would certainly be somebody who would turn up and take advantage of our openness. In today's world you don't know whom you can really trust. The amount of work going into the mango wine explains why the price is higher than that of a grape wine. Five kilograms of mangoes have to be hand processed to make one litre of mango wine. The taste however is far superior to other wines - the only wine that contains so many vitamins; all this has ultimately justified this investment. We are selling only direct to the public, cutting the middleman out. On the brochure, which I will leave with you, are our address details. You send us money; we send you the variety of mango wine you want."

The mango farm was a classic example of a migrant's determination to succeed with something at which others previously failed. This was the best-organised and cleanest farm I have ever seen. The key to success was the idea of a specialized farm and then the determination of a whole family to build on it with perseverance. This was a good demonstration of how the spirit of enterprise can create success in an environment that was not previously available to this family in Italy.

Our time at the Atherton Tablelands was running out; we had to get used to the idea of returning home. The Kennedy Highway led across forest highlands to Kuranda, a popular tourist destination just north of Cairns, which was the main tourist magnet of North Queensland. Before leaving the area, the forest reminded us one last time in the early morning hours that, of the 760 bird species in Australia, more than 300 could be found around lakes in the proximity of the rainforest of the tropical Tablelands.

Lake Eacham and Lake Barrine near Yungaburra, which we previously passed, were such bird-watching places. The catbird with its catlike sound, kingfishers and honeyeaters could be watched there relatively easily. The presence of riflebirds and frogmouths is an indication of how close Papua New Guinea is to North Queensland, because their species can also be found there.

Bird watching is one of nature's most difficult secrets to unravel; birds don't sit and wait for us to look at them. Long before we enter their territory, the catbird with its distinct mewing-cry has announced the intruder to all the other birds and creatures in a forest. Only time, patience and a total silence eventually outsmarts the bird world and convinces them to come out of their hiding places to eventually revert to their regular undisturbed daily pattern. Nature's warning messengers are not only understood by birds, but also by other species like wallabies, possums, and tree kangaroos.

KURANDA

Kuranda, a rainforest village, is located up on the mountain ridge of the coastal city of Cairns. Visitors to North Queensland come most of the time to see Kuranda. Surrounded by a world heritage listed rainforest on the Barron River, the town is home for many artists and markets. Its traditional inhabitants, the Djabuqay, local Aborigines, call it 'place of the platypus' ('Ngunbay')

The platypus is the most unique Australian mammal, a living fossil dating back about 15 million years. It lives in clean forest waters as well as in a basic residential burrow in the bank of a river. The platypus has a bill similar to that of a duck and short webbed legs. As a mammal it lays two side-by-side eggs stuck together and when hatched the young feed on milk from numerous ducts on the mother's abdomen.

According to legend, the platypus is a cross between a duck and a water rat. How much more peculiar could an animal be? The only one that could match it is another Australian species, the echidna.

Both platypus and echidna call Kuranda and the surroundings their home. They live in the ancient rainforests, the Barron River Gorge with its mighty falls, forest tracks with high up walking platforms close to the tree-tops, and even near the lookout opposite Barron Falls where, especially in the wet summer season, a mass of water hurtles down into an abyss disappearing between rock walls and encompassing rainforest.

Along the western banks of the Barron River runs an old railway line complete with historical steam train, which takes passengers from a beautifully established rainforest-station on a tour along the hillsides. Up in the sky above the forest's canopy, moving cabins of a 'Skyrail' can be seen through the trees. From the air, from forest platforms, and from the ground, people can experience a rainforest, something unique in the world. Celebrities such as the Queen have also paid their respects to the area.

Rainforests are an old ecological system of nature, where time has created a density of living forms in which the 'bigger' protects the 'smaller': the bigger plants compete in height keeping a moisture-cycle up to provide a cooler environment in which smaller species – both plants and animals – thrive underneath. A fine balance has been achieved in the rainforest.

A walk on a hot summer day into a 'rainforest cathedral' lets you experience its cooler conditions, which support life inside it. Birds, butterflies, ants, specialised wildlife, plant specimens like orchids, ferns, mosses, fallen tree-giants, young plant-life starting in the shadows of old species – all exist to support the rainforest's life cycles of decay and growth. For countless millions of years rainforests have survived right up until the present day; we have a responsibility to support such an ancient eco-system and not economize with it for short-term gains. There won't be another million years to recreate what we have changed.

Ultimately, in nature we all depend on each other; we cannot change something in it without effecting our own survival. It should be common knowledge that the bacteria which have built us, depend on the bacteria support base around us; when we change this support base, disease becomes the first consequence, leading eventually to changes that do not support living forms any more.

We are not the 'big tree' in the rainforest of life, but instead belong to the 'small creatures' on the ground. When we take the 'big trees' out, our protection is lost. The rainforest can still tell us today how living forms depend on each other. This information has always been simple and we are the ones who make it difficult through our push for progress thereby losing our connection with nature. Our destination is to prosper and then vanish; we are the ones that accelerate this course.

The silence and the voices in a rainforest should get us started in thinking better of our role in nature and come down from our self-declared domination to a more humble co-existence with the majority of other living forms. To aim at simplicity with all its solutions, has always been a 'hurdle' that we never seem to master, because it demands restrictions and not our much sought after expansion. Our intellect has gone astray with us putting everything at risk, both what we have created and finally, what created us.

What will nature wipe out first, the rainforest or us? At least in 2001 we could enter the remaining rainforest-pockets of Australia and develop a better understanding in our thoughts. It is not too late; we could still take that first step towards 'reconciliation' with nature. Today, the rainforest still keeps nature's longest living memories and greatest expressions, which is why I named it 'nature's cathedral'.

Lush rainforest

Tree ferns in the rainforest

Rainforest fauna

Nature's brilliant colours

Nature's Cathedral

(Poem-Martin Kari)

The city - concrete jungle - lies a long way back,
Single houses are far away,
A road - beaten track - fields, meadows - all have stopped.
In a green wall nature's stronghold rises out of its jungle.
Somewhere lower bush lightens,
allowing passage on foot into initial darkness.
Leaves, branches, lianas barricade the interior,
Little tree trunks lock-up space, whereas here and there
Large tree trunks rise up straight
holding a dark roof canopy high into the sky,
leaving little room for sunlight to shine through.
The catbird invisibly mews his penetrating warning,
An intruder has arrived in nature's rainforest cathedral.

Sounds are carried a long way,
high up through the canopy,
Everything has stopped and is watching from a hiding place,
On the ground: wallabies, possums, tree-kangaroos, bandicoots, cuscus,
brush-turkeys, goannas, pythons, tree-snakes, lizards, and geckos.
And in mid-area in young treetops: beetles, butterflies, spiders, and
insects.
Cicadas' chirping moves in waves across the forest cathedral
announcing the rain soon to come.
Some of nature's most colourful creatures: king parrots,
rainbow lorikeets, kingfishers, sunbirds, riflebirds, honeyeaters,
regent bowerbirds,
All watch the intruder from high up in the canopy.
All are present in the cathedral, but nothing can initially be seen.

Only when time returns with silence
do all creatures large and small start life's daily routines again,
moving, searching, feeding on what the rainforest holds,
sometimes playing, resting, waiting.
Silence of the permanent residents is then broken, telling
each other the different stories with sharp calls, long songs and noises.
A visitor can observe more near the ground
after the eye has adjusted to dim daylight.
Moist cooler air stores in a constant exchange.
The rain in the ground feeding hopeful young plant life
with fallen leaves, branches and trees.
Bird-nest ferns and stag-horns form leaf-cups high up in trees
to catch light and moisture.

A 'wait-a-while' creeper makes the hasty visitor
wait for a while to lick his wounds from nasty itchy contact.
Then a massive tree-trunk in the way stops the visitor
sending his eyes upwards to look how far he can see.
Some trees spread with flat triangular roots on the forest-floor
increasing the support of a jungle-giant on the ground.
Huge strangler figs often dominate other tree-giants
with their massive trunk roots
growing from the top of a host-tree all the way around.
When reaching the ground, the host-tree's fate is sealed,
The fig strangles the host.
Some trunk-roots of the strangler
become so huge that passages between allow you to walk through.

Old solid lianas also come down from old trees,
Often in loops to block a passage.
They never say 'swing on me'.
When crushing down from a dwindling height,
Only then will we know,

how firm, large and heavy they were,
endangering somebody underneath for sure.

Fungi, mosses, ants, snails often hide under leaves on the ground.
All life here is told not to make a 'mistake'.
And so the visitor is also bound to do,
When he wants to see something and stay safe from
the rainforest's natural defences -
wait-a-while, snakes, spiders, accidentally fallen branches.

Very few flowers develop in this darkness,
Umbrella trees with their long umbrella-formed leaves
specially attract lorikeets to their distinct red flower-studs
creating with the honey-licking lorikeets
an incredible colour paradise.
A goanna can rarely be seen,
often in a sunny spot soaking up the warmth.
When disturbed, they rush in haste
Up a tree-trunk.
Watching them already reveals
that they sense their direct environment
with their constant searching,
thin long tongue, an encounter with ancient pre-history.

In nature's cathedral many trees establish an existence
over a long period of time
and can therefore often be found today only in one place.
Rainforests in Australia are the oldest on earth
harbouring the richest variety in living forms
despite the small remaining forest pockets.
Black apple, red cedar, bunya pine,
trees still growing after hundreds of years into rainforest giants
tree ferns usually come up in penetrating light-corridors

giving the lower forest area a fine green shine
against the mostly dark-brown and dark-green forest shades.
Lower areas of a rainforest can harbour a watercourse.

Palms near a water-flow add a tropical image to the forest.

Water usually leaves a forest
starting a journey through countryside,
mostly without the protection of the forest.
Only a constant supply from the forest
gives a river the start for its journey.
Without it, a river ceases to exist.
Time in a rainforest cathedral seems to stop.
Birds from the high canopy tell with their voices
when morning and nightfall arrive.
In the night's darkness many rainforest residents waken to life,
possums, geckos, bandicoots, bats, seeking the cooler hours.
To leave the rainforest cathedral during the day
Is to bring back the open heat of the land.

The rainforest is a cathedral,
a quiet place, where high trees support its 'roof',
creating a huge dome under which life finds protection.
Visiting a rainforest cathedral gives us back
Nature's very basic strength for our body and mind.
We have an obligation to preserve what is left of the rainforest
So that future generations can also experience this paradise on earth.
When leaving the rainforest cathedral
the green wall of nature's jungle
remains behind unchanged.
Meadows, fields, beaten tracks, roads bring us closer
to single houses again and finally
back to our own jungle creation,
The city – concrete jungle.

Back in Kuranda Village, Aborigines staged dance performances several times a day to give others a window into their bygone world. Their tradition to live and act within a traditional community has restricted the individual's chance to break out; in other words, the 'clan' kept everybody together, but also prevented the individual from advancing independently.

Indigenous dancers at Kuranda, North Queensland

A timely African proverb says: 'If you want to go fast, go it alone; if you want to go far, you have to go it together'. Was this going-together rule the secret of Aborigines' survival for tens of thousands of years? What is the difference between their lives and ours - mainly that of the Europeans? Are Europeans collective individuals, who have offset community traditions in the past in order to 'go fast'? History will have to go much further before we can tell who is wrong or right.

Stylish shops in Kuranda village exhibited work from people who had often chosen an alternative lifestyle; by producing only what they think is needed for a less stressful life away from the city and its people. Most artwork displayed here could stand up to comparison from anywhere else - timber-works, pottery, jewellery, batiste-work, shoe-works and speciality-booths, also a Bavarian Weisswurst-Sauerkraut-German beer outlet. From its backyard position the café was not allowed to reach the main street with its full-of-fire music. As our daughter-in-law was Australian and had not yet been to Germany, we gave it a try so she could experience a bit of this German cheerfulness in front of a sausage, sauerkraut and beer. Everything went well here in North Queensland so that we were ready to move on to Cairns, down on the coast.

CAIRNS AND SURROUNDINGS

The beauty of Cairns

The road rapidly descended in serpentines from the coastal mountains. A modern city received us, a major tourist Mecca of Australia. The cityscape that greeted us was interlaced with tropical greenery. Founded in 1876 as a service-town for the goldfields, Cairns has evolved from a rough frontier outpost, where the pubs nearly outnumbered the people, to an international cosmopolitan destination.

International airlines bring tourists from all over the world. As we arrived, a huge aircraft took off from the airport cruising over the bay in front of the city, taking a full load of tourists back to their overseas homes. Technology like this aircraft stands out much more in a totally green oasis; two different worlds seem to have met here.

After a holiday, some rich tourists even decide to settle in and around Cairns, taking no time at all to unwind and slip into the easier lifestyle. All year round the days are warm, the nights are balmy with endless possibilities of things to do. This makes holidaying in North Queensland an experience of a lifetime. The more people who find this out, the more the demand rises which in turn puts up prices in many ways so that already in 2001, holidaying in resorts and hotels was quite expensive. With a population of 130 000, Cairns has pushed developments further north along the Coral Sea to places like Port Douglas, Mossman, Daintree, Cape Tribulation, and Cooktown.

Cooktown is also the home of Queensland's tropical emblem, the Cooktown orchid. Growing to half a metre, it is one of the most beautiful specimens of the orchid family. Its flowers are deep carmine and purple with a white throat. It lives for many years. The Cooktown orchid is a stunning natural beauty ambassador of North Queensland.

Cooktown orchid

Daintree is also known for its World Heritage listed rainforest. However, controversies arose between the push for development and the conservation movement, resulting over the years in the construction of a road and properties, which were built into the rainforest with the proviso that no tree is removed. Undoubtedly this was a world first, that properties have been built in a rainforest with the assistance of helicopters from the air. It shouldn't be forgotten however that a home like this would be out of reach for most people. Money has started to play its role here also. It remains to be seen for how long Daintree will maintain its unspoilt character in the face of slow changes allowed to happen from time to time.

Also here we have to become more determined to preserve what is left in a natural environment and not give in to money considerations; if we don't turn 'green' in time, there will not be enough green left to stand up for. Yellow-white sand beaches, poisonous-green rainforests right to the beach edge, blue-green Coral Sea, a deep blue sky with patchy white clouds developing during the day – all this and most of the time no human settlements yet.

In varying distances from the coast are other holiday destinations - islands of the Great Barrier Reef Marine Park. Ferries and cruise ships connect to the islands, rated the richest and largest Marine Park in the world; they also show the colourful marine-life of corals and fish. Diving in the Coral Sea always has to be undertaken with caution, as there are an untold number of dangerous sea-creatures sharing the underwater world. Swimming is possible only in fully protected beach areas. It should never be forgotten that the coast is also the home of the fierce salt-water crocodile. Nature's balance always delivers 'good' and 'bad' together. The 'bad' usually helps to keep the 'good' strong.

On the land up to Mossman the road was hard; further north a beaten track took over. During the wet season in summer this track becomes impassable. North of Cooktown there ceased to be anything that even resembled a road. Experience with a four-wheel drive vehicle and the use of caution ensures that, in the north, new adventures to many sights of interest are possible. Such a tour should be considered only during winter, the dry season, because not only does the wet make touring very difficult, there is also the added summer heat.

BLACK MOUNTAIN NATIONAL PARK

I'd like to mention one sight 30 km. north of Cooktown – Black Mountain National Park, an intriguing formation made up of a giant pile of black granite boulders. Where in the world have they come from? The boulders sit only on their own mountain and are to be found nowhere else nearby. Aborigines have found their answer to this natural phenomenon in many legends and stories passed on from generation to generation. Tales of explorers who were said to have visited the mountain, entered its tunnels and never returned accentuate mysteries surrounding the mountain. All visitors are advised to remain within a specific viewing area.

Black Mountain National Park - North Queensland

In the dense rainforests a cassowary might eventually be sighted, a bird similar to the emu, but more colourful. It has strong three-claw feet, dense black plumage and a blue neck with pink spots, and a head that changes to white with a brownish crest and a strong beak. A cassowary can be aggressive; the first indication of its presence in a dense forest is a low rumble like the sound of an approaching truck - the noise the bird makes when it meets something unfamiliar.

When approached, the bird usually keeps quiet and watches first. If an intruder comes close enough, the cassowary will then stand up tall, raise all its feathers and give a loud hiss to scare the intruder off. From then on the bird can become unpredictable, especially during breeding season. The cassowary can also be found in Papua New Guinea, which indicates a prehistoric connection between North Queensland and Papua.

When talking about tropical places, we should not forget to mention the typical fruit belonging to it. On the Tablelands we saw mangoes but there are a few others such as caramba or 'five corner fruit' (its star-shaped yellow slices make an attractive addition to fruit salad), custard apple, cherimoya (its skin is composed of a distinctive overlapping fleshy green petal effect); pineapple which is more commonly known, rambutan (a close relative of the lychee with a sweet-sour white core in a hairy reddish shell). The name rambutan comes from the Malay 'rambut' meaning hair. One more tropical fruit is the paw-paw, also known as papaya in Spain. All of these tropical fruits are primarily rich in vitamin C, mainly because of the plentiful sun they receive.

When it comes to shopping, Cairns Central Shopping Centre could hardly be missed. During hot summer days, lot of locals spend some time out of their day here in the air-conditioned building complexes, which become in many ways a meeting point.

Undersea World Aquarium, marine boat harbours, boat tours through mangroves on the shores of Cairns and protected beaches along the northern suburbs give plenty of opportunities for a relaxed holiday.

Effective sun protection should never be forgotten, as Queensland is the skin cancer centre of the world! It takes only moments of intensive midday sun to develop the beginnings of a harmful skin cancer, sometimes surfacing decades later. Nobody deserves to get skin cancer from a holiday all because of simple neglect.

Our tour continued southwards from Cairns. Shortly after the southern suburbs on the foot of the coastal mountain ranges, there was the railway station. All we could see from the road was an endless queue of people waiting for the chance to travel the scenic tour through rainforest mountain slopes up to Kuranda across the bridge over Stoney Creek Falls.

The Kuranda Scenic Railway climbs across awesome ravines and gorges through exotic vegetation and past the hiding places of endangered rainforest creatures. The trip has been made for over 100 years, so that travellers can observe what only forest residents have seen over a period of time.

Scenic railway to Kuranda - North Queensland

The 'Skyrail', another way to explore the ancient rainforest wilderness in comfort, starts north of Cairns in Caravonica. This unique trip from high above the forest's canopy will take your breath away. Both the Scenic Railway and the Skyrail are popular tourist destinations; it requires good timing not to miss such an experience because often too many tourists have arrived.

Skyrail over rainforest - Cairns to Kuranda, North Queensland

Mount Bartle Frere, Queensland's highest mountain, lies inland on the coastal plain and is completely covered by rainforest. Despite sunny weather, the higher region of the mountain was dipped in thick cloud cover, surrounding only the mountain peak. Anybody taking on the mountain with its steep hazardous rainforest slopes should eventually break through the clouds near the top and have a bird's eye view. They should now be able to experience the Coral Sea to the east, the Tablelands to the west, mountains covered with rainforests in the north and south. Before starting such an expedition, thorough planning would be needed. It would also be recommended not to undertake this tour alone, because of a hazardous climb involving many hours and no overnight accommodation up there; it is wild territory.

1800 kilometres still separated us from our hometown Caboolture in the southeast corner of Queensland.

Time reminded us to get back on 'the road to Nitmiluk' and close the circle from where we had started.

SOUTHBOUND

TOWNSVILLE

The weekend back in Townsville got into full swing with a cabinet-making job in the house of our son Risto. He had, during his time at the Darwin Airbase, acquired mahogany planks from an old grown tree, which had to be removed in the wake of a development project. The planks were thick and wide enough to make a big tabletop out of one piece. A proper frame and four legs underneath had to carry the heavy top section. The table was so heavy that we had to work inside the house in the dining room with the table in its fixed position. The solid mahogany timber was already worth something on its own, not to mention what the finished 2 x 1 metre table would be worth.

This was another step in a younger generation's own household, very much in our family tradition i.e. what you can do yourself, do it only once and do it right. Real quality and value is not easy to come by in today's consumer world. Quality you can produce yourself gives you a special pride and a good feeling that you have also substantially saved and you won't need to change your own work. People claiming they cannot do something, have in real terms never started to do it, cutting out the necessary learning curve, which applies to everything that we do, whether it is in 'theory' or 'praxis'. We like to go one or the other way in doing something instead of embarking at an earlier stage on both, praxis and theory. Praxis should tell us about the required theory; there are more theoretical practitioners than practical theorists around! A roast joint dinner late Sunday on the new table became, after a successful team-effort, the best farewell we could have had from Townsville.

Family excursion in North Queensland

HOMEWARD BOUND

Early next morning before dawn, my wife and I headed off, southbound on the Bruce Highway. A stylish country town lay in the Burdekin River plains, overlooking vast sugarcane fields. The town of Ayr in the north is built away from the Burdekin River avoiding the river's seasonal floods; its satellite township of Home Hill in the south is also away from the river for the same reason.

Another 115 kilometres further south, the town of Bowen lies on the coast. It is a typical small Queensland town with its Queensland-style houses raised from the ground with verandas around and the same high pitched roof, surrounded also by marvellous tropical gardens. The town has given Queensland its own mango variety, the Bowen mango, known for its quality without the stringiness of some other varieties, making tasting a pure pleasure. Bowen mangoes are extensively grown and their spherical reddish-green leaf-canopy supplies a distinct image to the area. Mountains, forests and bush again grew closer to the coast, looking now during winter rather dry and less exuberant than in the north. Grasslands along the coast looked especially dry with their yellow-brown colour.

Proserpine represented the gateway to the nearby Whitsunday Islands and the Great Barrier Reef. Islands like Hayman, Hamilton, Lindeman, and Brampton offer first class holiday standards in a pristine maritime island-environment of beaches, forests, crystal-clear Coral Sea, and resorts with amazing luxury at amazing prices, which make some people reconsider their options.

One of the many islands off the coast of North Queensland

The region's Barrier Reef is an underwater wonder world hopefully staying unspoilt for a long time to come. The run-off from polluted rivers and agricultural activities of settlements along the coast endanger the delicate marine life, especially in the coral reef. At least the present awareness of such a danger promises that the right measures to save this World Heritage listed Marine Park might eventually prevail. Many people arriving here from around the world experience this reef wonder world and contribute significantly to the local economy, ensuring that conservation efforts become even more of a priority.

Further south lay Mackay, a major loading port for the Newlands Coal Mine, which is located inland. Open-cut mining in numerous places supplies pit-coal to many parts of the world. One of these mines is at Blackwater. Coal layers are so deep that they could supply the world for the next thousand years. Considering today's environmental requirements, a reasonable suggestion is a cautious approach in exploiting natural resources.

An over-sized statue of a bull announces Rockhampton, the city centre of a large cattle area. Depending on climate and market conditions, fortunes here have also been made and lost in the past, a standard in many other agricultural centres of Queensland and elsewhere in Australia. People in the countryside are, for such reasons, resilient to life's ups and downs, which are a constant companion for them.

Besides cattle, Rockhampton has also developed its own tourist Mecca on Great Keppel Island. The Great Barrier Reef extends to this area. Major mining areas lie inland from here. One of these, Mount Morgan, is said to be the biggest open-cut mine in the world. Huge machinery constantly cuts the coal and loads it into giant trucks and endless rail-lorries and transports the coal to Yeppoon on the coast for shipping.

Still further inland are Emerald and Sapphire, mineral centres, where besides sapphires, agates, petrified wood and many others, the most beautiful opals in the world can be found. Friends of ours from New Zealand had spent a number of years seriously fossicking for gold, sapphires and opals around Emerald in search of the big fortune of their lives. Many people try to develop a lifestyle out of it, but only a few manage to attain a good living standard. Reaching for a fortune with the help of metal detectors and hand digging in extreme summer temperatures turns it for most, into an illusion or an adventure.

When people vie in search of a fortune, tight competition can be expected. Jealousy, cheating, disappointment, politics and, very occasionally, success make this a hard life. The ones leaving with little or no success are often lost in a city environment and find going back to a normal daily life very difficult. No longer are they living with the excitement of finding their 'pot of gold' and life can seem boring.

Our friends from New Zealand got caught in this 'game'. After spending years of their lives searching for gold, sapphires and opals they returned to their previous life. They did keep however the knowledge of the region and the exceptional stories of the people they met. It is a pity that these people cannot write about their experiences so that their many stories stay with them. A 'gold-digger's' life has its highlights just like every other life; lessons are learnt, and it challenges everybody one way or another, sooner or later. From that point of view, aren't we all in some sense 'gold-diggers'?

Forests covered the Dividing Ranges all the way to the west; valleys and their creeks crossed the Capricorn Highway, going gradually over into the outback further west.

Back in Rockhampton, a sign on the roadside - Tropic of Capricorn - informed us that we were leaving the tropics. From now on sub-tropical territory lay ahead with a climate mostly lower in humidity, which translates into a reduced cyclone danger – always a threat in the tropics during the summer. To understand the impact of a cyclone on a community, it is worth mentioning that in 2006 a 300km/hour wind of cyclonic fury completely devastated Innisfail in the north along with its banana plantations. From far beyond the affected area the nation pulled together and helped to rebuild Innisfail, so the many residents affected could still call it home.

Shortly before Gladstone our touring day came to an end in a caravan park at the small town of Mount Larcom. While we stopped for the night, the trucks and goods trains on the nearby road and railway line remained busy, which didn't help much in getting a good night's sleep.

The caravan park was very popular for an overnight stay as it was well set up. A decent shower in a caravan park after a day of travelling was always a welcome respite.

At first daylight we were up and back on the road. Gladstone, the next major town, is another major shipping port for pit-coal from the inland's rich open cut coalmines. T he town has also developed businesses to service the mining industry.

When driving further south towards Bundaberg the road passes through Childers, a small town that underwent a terrible tragedy. There was a strong reminder of the backpacker tragedy still weighing upon this small community, from when their beautiful hostel was deliberately set on fire claiming a number of young overseas backpackers' lives. The hostel has been rebuilt, once more accommodating visitors who want to experience life in a small Queensland country town. Backpackers often come with a work visa, picking fruit during their holiday. All the wounds of the past seemed to have healed; the confidence in the friendly population of Childers has returned, renewed and strong out of the ashes.

Bundaberg is the centre of a sugarcane area, the most southern productive region of Queensland. Small exemptions were around the Sunshine Coast, where early Finnish settlers had cleared the land and cultivated sugarcane with great effort. It couldn't be missed; the further north the fields were located, the higher and denser the sugarcane stood. During the dry summers in the early 2000's the cane didn't reach a proper harvesting height, thereby forcing farmers to abandon farming so far south. Today's generation has also largely abandoned those early farming efforts, allowing the cane fields to lie fallow more and more often. A Memorial Park on its own 'Finlandia Road' today remembers the sacrifices of those early Finnish pioneers.

Coming back to our tour, we passed through Maryborough, where the biggest sand-island of the world lies off the coast, separated only by a narrow strait from the mainland. Fraser Island is World Heritage listed and is one of the main tourist draw-cards in South-East Queensland. Constant strong winds and currents from the south have built four sand-islands over millions of years along the eastern coast of Southern Queensland. Fraser Island is the biggest of them all. The other three are located on the shores near Brisbane: North Stradbroke, Moreton, and Bribie Island.

They all owe their existence to the Pacific and are covered with hillsides, dense forests, natural lakes of fresh water, and coloured sands on steep cliffs. There is a constant temptation to exploit the islands' rich mineral sands; large deposits of rutile, and other minerals essential for metallurgic processes are hidden in the sand. Only on Stradbroke and Moreton Island have limited mining activities been allowed; environmentalists work hard to prevent an expansion. The pressure to exploit these mineral deposits is growing because there are only a few other deposits known in the world.

Some Australian wildlife has remained on the islands despite increased pressure from visitors and limited residential developments. Dingos, the Australian wild dogs, can always be sighted on Fraser Island. They can become intrusive when people feed them. The dogs can develop aggressive tendencies and take whatever they believe they deserve if somebody suddenly stops feeding them. All sorts of incidents and stories have emerged from this wrong feeding attitude towards the dingo. As a better understanding for the natural living conditions of dingos has come into effect, feeding is now forbidden not only of dingos but of any other wildlife as well. In this way their instincts for finding food in their natural habitat don't get confused.

The Pacific side of Fraser Island is 120 kilometres long, running in a straight line, making it a paradise for long beach walks. Mainly because of the sharks' presence, swimming is not recommended. All in all, Fraser Island is a natural paradise for holidaymakers, but not in too large a number. Around Christmas, when everybody in the country tries to get away from the summer heat in town, it can happen that large numbers of visitors turn up on the island. Keen four-wheel drivers occasionally cross the strait on low tide, but it is more common to use the ferry from Harvey Bay.

SUNSHINE COAST - BACK HOME

The journey homewards is said to go faster the nearer you get and this was our experience. Once we passed the lovely small country town of Gympie on its hilly sides, the Sunshine Coast came in sight soon after, with Noosa Head Rock sitting directly on the coast. We had arrived in familiar territory again. After having seen so many different landscapes and people, everything familiar seemed to have a new look. At first everything probably appeared a bit smaller, whether distances, the nearby mountain slopes of the Sunshine Hinterland or the local places.

Small settlements followed and the number of vehicles on the road increased. Golden sand-beaches stretched along the coast from Noosa in the north to Caloundra in the south, where residential houses and holiday resorts competed for space and the tourist dollar. They have so quickly made this region into a world-class tourist destination.

The Sunshine Coast fortunately still trails its rival tourist centre – the Gold Coast, located 200 kilometres further south past the capital Brisbane. This makes it therefore a more private place for a holiday. Underwater World ocean aquarium in Mooloolaba is one of its drawcards, where all creatures of the Pacific coast can be watched. Observers are moved along on a conveyor belt through a glass tunnel under the aquarium, surrounded by sharks, mantas, sawfish, colourful coral reefs, and incredible coloured fish. A very interesting seal training show can also be watched from a stage in front of a rocky pool.

High up on a ridge overlooking the coast lies the small town of Montville, which has attracted into its lush green highland environment, hobbyists and artists who enjoy working away from the rush of the coast. Visitors to the area can enjoy rainforest walks, waterfalls, local and overseas speciality restaurants, and country-style accommodations for every budget. For most of the year the climate here is more moderate, leaving the summer sultriness down on the coast. Even wine cultivation has been established with the result that a few quality wines are found here, thanks to an Italian family who had started a vineyard, which goes back generations.

The relative density of the population in South East Queensland has created its own cultural expressions in arts, gastronomy, paintings, and literature plus an unstoppable push for development right across many fields within this rapidly growing community. Fifteen hundred people per week are said to have moved to South East Queensland over the last 25 years, seeking sunshine and a lifestyle in a rich natural environment. Consequently this has recently added to higher living costs, especially in the housing affordability area. A house of thirty thousand dollars in 1981 cost ten times more in 2006, mostly because of an increase in the population, not only from within Australia but also from overseas. Many wealthy people have established another home here in Queensland, where we are spoilt by the nature and the weather.

The striking volcanic rock formations of the Glasshouse Mountains are one of the most beautiful natural areas found anywhere in the world. When we passed close by, the mountains overlooked the surrounding rich farming land of pineapples, avocado, macadamia, and passionfruit. From our property we can see the tops of the rugged rocky ancient volcano-core mountains.

On this last leg we decided to leave the Bruce Highway and take on a slower pace when coming closer to home. Isn't it a good way to gradually re-enter daily life after an experience so different from home and catch up first with some familiar sites? On the side of the road there were stalls of farmers selling their fresh products from their property behind. A cold pineapple drink from freshly picked and ripened pineapples helped to restore some of our energy for the moment.

While driving through familiar territory, Australia Zoo came into sight on the scenic road near the Glasshouse Mountains. Refreshed, we could easily make a stop at the natural zoo and welcome Australia's wildlife closer to home. We have seen the place developing from a tiny park with only a few wildlife specimens into a large internationally recognised enterprise. The driving force behind the zoo was Steve Irwin, also known as the 'Crocodile Hunter'. Yes, this corner of the world is the home of the 'Crocodile Hunter', who helped to put Australia with its unique wildlife on the world map.

In 2006, Steve Irwin unfortunately became a victim of his beloved environment in his drive for nature's conservation; an encounter with a stingray on our Pacific shores killed him. His legend however lives on in Australia Zoo, where his wife and two children continue the great idea of bringing our nature closer to the people, so a better understanding of conservation can be nurtured. Kangaroos and wallabies can be watched in the wide park as they move on the lawns freely between people. A touch with the hand will tell everybody how fine, soft and smooth a kangaroo's skin is.

During the day, Harriet, the oldest known giant tortoise living on earth, warmed her massive rounded shell in the sun, not moving much any more at the age of 175 years. In earlier times Harriet was brought in from the Galapagos Islands off the west coast of Ecuador. Crocodiles are kept in safe ponds and one of the highlights of the Zoo used to be the demonstration of the 'Crocodile Hunter' as he played daredevil games with them, obviously knowing his crocodiles well.

Other fauna abounds like snakes, lizards, parrots, and birds. Birds of prey can be watched in the natural environment of a beautifully established garden of Eden, which also shows the rich flora of palms, cycads, trees and many flowers. The colourful Australian birds have their own sanctuary in a totally enclosed tropical garden, which visitors could enter through a safety double-door corridor in order to watch the birds directly in their natural rainforest environment.

The park has grown from very humble beginnings into a major destination for tourists and locals and it has given the tiny country town of Beerwah a boost in employment opportunities. An extension to the park occurred in an environmentally friendly way; a big nearby property of old established macadamia nut trees was incorporated without changes to the plantation, giving the park an additional special appearance with this old grown dense tree canopy. A very firm determination has to be behind a development like the Australia Zoo to make it succeed in a 'sleepy' country place, away from the main tourist attractions of South East Queensland. Without doubt this is the merit of Steve's driving spirit of enterprise. Success in Australia has its tough sides, but then also very sweet ones. It is a privilege to call this region home, and it is always a new experience when returning and finding out how beautiful it still is.

When we arrived home we were greeted by a shining example of Murphy's Law – 'whatever can go wrong, will go wrong!' Our homecoming was not as sweet as it could be. One particular surprise had developed during our absence: son Micki had his first driving lessons with our other car and as a consequence the car was not on the property any more, but in a place where it was supposed to be fixed quickly and cheaply. At least son Micki was okay. There is rarely anything that can't be fixed. Our newly acquired experiences outweighed past hiccups allowing the immediate future to progress in a mainly positive direction.

14 000 kilometres on the 'road to Nitmiluk' lay behind us. A big tour-circle was successfully completed and home was still the castle we again loved most. Only by going out and returning to this place we call home, is it possible to rediscover its values after having seen so much.

EPILOGUE

Mission accomplished — and what a mission! In order to experience and understand Australia first hand as a continent and country with its unique nature and people, we had set out on our journey.

Our family had arrived in Australia as migrants 20 years earlier. 'Road to Nitmiluk' is not our first and only experience with the fifth continent, but definitely another comprehensive one. On the way we met city-folk, tourists, outback battlers and most of all the Aborigines, the oldest migrant residents of the continent. Nature here is quite simply unique; nowhere else can a comparison to it be found. With careful observation its harsh beauty can only inspire us; much of it is hidden, revealing itself only to the attentive eye.

Being in the neighbourhood of Antarctica, Australia, as the oldest part of the world is also a front-runner in environmental responses because of its sensitive ecology. Any environmental impact from around the world registers first in the Antarctica and its Australian neighbour.

During this tour I have described the unchanged beauty of Australia, which human activities couldn't change, thankfully because of the concentrated population in only a few regions. Our tour-circle on the road to Nitmiluk closed after 14 000 kilometres in the southeast corner of Queensland. A good preparation and courage were needed to travel this road as well as an experienced touring team of just two, and including that bit of luck often required in life; all this made the essential companions.

ABOUT THE AUTHOR

Born in Transylvania during World War II, life has kept Martin Kari on a life's journey to Europe, the Orient, Africa, South America and finally Australia. Education at various levels didn't stop him from going to the best knowledge source of all - real people - to learn more about the real world. Raising a family of three boys and three girls with his beautiful Finnish wife, Arja, Martin finally settled his family in Australia, where they successfully established their home.

BACK COVER BLURB

Nitmiluk, a National Park in the Northern Territory, is on an Australian road leading through Southern Queensland, the Outback, the Northern Territory, the Red Centre, the Top End, North Queensland Tablelands and back to the beginning in South East Queensland – 14 000 kilometres by car closed this tour-circle.

As new Australian citizens, the author, Martin Kari, and his wife Arja went on this journey to Nitmiluk in order to deepen their knowledge of their new homeland. With the experience of journeys in other parts of the world, they found this journey special and unique: moving from a pulsing city-life on the east coast into the dead silence of the Outback.

Its dry image hides Australia's special fauna and flora. However there are many unexpected paradise-oases along with great distances, rich colours, grasslands, bush, rainforests, flat country, vast mountainous areas, rich farming land, semi-deserts, creeks, rivers, endless coastlines and beaches harbouring a magnificent marine life. And not least of all, there are the people of Australia.

Landscapes from around the world can be found right here in Australia and therefore it is no surprise to also find people from all parts of the world calling Australia home.

www.ingramcontent.com/pod-product-compliance
Lightning Source LLC
Chambersburg PA
CBHW031122020426
42333CB00012B/185